VANCOUVER CANUCKS

The Silver Edition

WRITTEN BY SEAN ROSSITER

FOREWORD BY JIM ROBSON

A WHITECAP / OPUS BOOK

On October 9, 1970, CKNW broadcast the Vancouver Canucks' first NHL game. As we begin our 25th NHL broadcast season with the Canucks, CKNW/98 is proud to celebrate our 25 year association. CKNW congratulates the Vancouver Canucks in their spectacular run to the '94 Stanley Cup finals, and wishes them the very best in their pursuit to bring the Stanley Cup to Vancouver.

CKNW/98
B.C.'S MOST LISTENED TO RADIO STATION
and Talked to

It seems like only yesterday we were living the excitement of our '94 run to the Stanley Cup – one of the most exhilarating chapters in the Vancouver Canucks' history. My memories of those electrifying games are still fresh, memories I know we all share. The path to the Stanley Cup held one challenge

Arthur Griffiths and Greg Adams celebrate a '94 playoff moment.

A memorable occasion such as this provides an opportunity to reflect on our past: Where did it all begin? What were the events that shaped our present team? Who were the people who made it all possible?

This book is witness to the players, management, opponents and loyal fans who contributed

after another, and we met them all, reaching the edge of triumph. Although we didn't bring the Cup home to Vancouver, we were all winners in our hearts.

As we begin the 1994–95 season, we enter our 25th year in the NHL – our silver anniversary.

to the character and success of our team today. Vancouver Canucks – The Silver Edition captures many of the highlights and special memories of the past 24 seasons of Canuck history. What better testimony of our team, then and now.

ARTHUR GRIFFITHS
*Chairman, Chief Executive Officer and Governor
Vancouver Canucks*

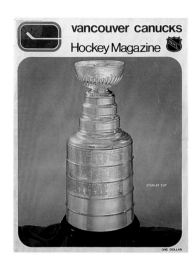

The Vancouver Canucks' first-game program,
October 9, 1970.

Published and produced by Opus Productions Inc.,
300 West Hastings Street, Vancouver, British Columbia, Canada V6B 1K6

Distributed in Canada by Whitecap Books Limited, 351 Lynn Avenue, North Vancouver, British Columbia, Canada V7J 2C4

First Published in 1994

10 9 8 7 6 5 4 3 2 1

Canadian Cataloguing in Publication Data
Rossiter, Sean, 1946-
      Vancouver Canucks

        Includes bibliographical references and index.
        ISBN 0-921926-12-X

        1. Vancouver Canucks (Hockey team)—Pictorial works. 2.
Vancouver Canucks (Hockey team)—History.   I. Title
GV848. V35R67 1994   796.962'64'0971133   C94-910831-6

Printed and bound in Canada
by H. MacDonald Printing Company

Front cover: clockwise, starting upper left: *Trevor Linden,*
Pavel Bure, Kirk McLean, Cliff Ronning.

Back cover: clockwise, starting upper left: *Orland Kurtenbach,*
Gary Smith, Thomas Gradin, Patrik Sundstrom, Stan Smyl,
Harold Snepsts, Curt Fraser, Tiger Williams.

Facing page: *A "Hall of Fame" lineup: hockey sticks from*
past and present Canucks, assembled from the private
collection of "Superfan" Andrew Castell.

Table of Contents

Foreword: By Jim Robson   6

Chapter One: The Playoffs, April 18 – May 24, 1994   10

Chapter Two: Black Tuesday, 1970–1974   26

Chapter Three: Building a Contender, 1974–1982   38

Chapter Four: The Legend, 1982–1986   52

Chapter Five: Stealing Pat Quinn, 1986–1994   66

Chapter Six: The Stanley Cup Final, May 28 – June 14, 1994   86

The Future   104

Statistical Summary   108

Bibliography and Acknowledgements   112

Superpest, Cracklin' Rosie, Captain Kurt, Cleaver, Schmautzie, Suitcase, Steamer, Tiger, Lurch, Haaaa-rold, King Richard, Captain Kirk and The Russian Rocket ...Those nicknames belong to hockey players — colourful, successful athletes who have become part of the history of the Vancouver Canucks.

Granted, it is not a long history. Fifty years, if you go back to the team's founding in the old Pacific Coast Hockey League. Half that many if you take in only the years Vancouver has been part of the National Hockey League, hockey's greatest league.

For years the Vancouver Canucks were a team of limited success, a team that seemed incapable of building any traditions or recording any noteworthy achievements. For many years, all the Canucks could count on was a loyal following. Even that deserted them in some of their worst seasons.

Those fans who waited years to cheer Vancouver's own NHL team will never forget the first season. They'll tell you about the exploits of a little centre named Andre Boudrias – "Superpest" – so popular a song was written about him. That first Canuck team was led by "Captain Kurt" – Orland Kurtenbach – a star in the team's first-ever

From the beginning: Jim Robson and Pat Quinn, some 24 seasons ago.

win over the Toronto Maple Leafs, a team the Canucks still find ways to beat. And who could forget "Cracklin' Rosie" Paiement, who was at his best against the Stanley Cup champion Boston Bruins. He beat them one night when his third goal of the game was a last-minute game-winner. Another night in Boston Rosie made headlines by giving Bobby Orr a black eye that postponed a series of television commercials.

After the eventful first year, the Canucks ran into some hard times, but the fans could still cheer "Schmautzie"— the feisty, hard-shooting winger from Saskatoon, Bobby Schmautz. Don "Cleaver" Lever arrived as one first-round draft pick who lived up to his billing.

A highlight of the team's first decade was the 86-point first-place finish in 1975. Coach Phil Maloney kept calling on much-travelled goaltender Gary "Suitcase" Smith, who played a gruelling 72 games, winning 32 with six shutouts, and should have won the Hart Trophy.

Hall of Fame builder Jake Milford and Hall of Fame character Harry Neale were in charge by the late '70s. There was a Swedish invasion, led by solid defenceman Lars "Lurch" Lindgren and slick centre Thomas Gradin, who became one of the best Canucks of all time. The fans were chanting "Haaaa-rold" as a salute to Harold Snepsts, whose popularity became legendary. "The Steamer" quickly built a big following, too; any hockey fan could appreciate the efforts of Stan Smyl.

The cheers were loudest in 1982 when the Canucks went all the way to the Stanley Cup final. "King Richard" Brodeur provided spectacular goaltending and coach Roger Neilson provided inspiration by waving a white towel on the end of a hockey stick one night at Chicago Stadium, turning a moment of protest into a Vancouver hockey tradition. Add the likes of the colourful Dave "Tiger" Williams, Darcy Rota, Curt Fraser and Ivan Boldirev, and Vancouver fans had plenty to cheer about.

But it has been the '90s that have provided the brightest chapter in the growing history of the Canucks. The Pat Quinn era has brought long-awaited respect, a 100-point season, the finest playoff in the team's history and its greatest player, Pavel Bure, "The Russian Rocket" – the long-awaited superstar. With "Captain Kirk" McLean brilliant in the nets and Trevor Linden

finally comfortable at centre, the Canucks went right down to the final seconds of a seventh game in a most-memorable Stanley Cup final before losing by a single goal to the heavily favoured New York Rangers.

I have been privileged to watch the Vancouver Canucks of the Pacific Coast League play at the old PNE Forum. I called the first game at the Pacific Coliseum. And I was in the broadcast booth at Madison Square Garden for the unforgettable Game 7 of the 1994 Stanley Cup final. I've enjoyed following the Canucks every season in between. So I feel like a witness to the history of the Vancouver Canucks. In devouring every word and picture in this book, I have lived it all once again. I recommend the same pleasure to the many loyal Canuck fans and everyone who loves the great game of hockey.

JIM ROBSON
Galiano Island, B.C.
September 1, 1994

Lord Stanley of Preston's bowl, as it looked when it last resided in Vancouver. First competed for in 1893, the Stanley Cup is the oldest trophy in North American professional sports. The Vancouver Millionaires won it in 1915 with a team whose regular players, led by the great Fred "Cyclone" Taylor, all were inducted into the Hockey Hall of Fame.

The Vancouver Canucks' 24th National Hockey League campaign finished as a disappointment: 84 regular season games with 41 wins, 40 losses and three ties. Twelfth overall, second in the Pacific Division, the team had stumbled, after first-place finishes in 1992 and 1993. Now the playoffs. The Vancouver–Calgary rivalry beckoned and the unexpected classic that unfolded opened up unimagined possibilities.

The Playoffs

To all Canuck fans on the edge of their seats, Hockey Night in Canada *provided this bird's-eye view of Kirk McLean's Save of the Century in Calgary, Game 7 overtime.*

Facing page: *Every photo of Kirk McLean is a goaltending clinic: he is always balanced, square to the shooter and keeps his stick flat on the ice. He gives away nothing.*

GAME 7: APRIL 30, 1994. SADDLEDOME, CALGARY. STANLEY CUP QUARTERFINALS, ABOUT 11:40 INTO OVERTIME.

It's simple. If Kirk McLean doesn't make the Save of the Century, Vancouver's springtime Stanley Cup joyride is over before it has begun. Like so many great scoring chances, this one starts at the opposite end of the rink, with the Canucks doing everything but putting the puck in the net:

Murray Craven's line has been buzzing around the Calgary net for most of a shift. So relentless is the pressure that Flames goalie Mike Vernon twice tries to lift the puck out of his zone himself. Jyrki Lumme takes the second attempt off the glass and keeps it in, moving the puck up to Craven.

The Flames get a big jump out of their own zone when, suddenly, the rebound from Craven's goalmouth pass comes off the right boards directly to Flames winger Gary Roberts. Canuck defenceman Dana Murzyn, who has no choice but to commit himself when the puck goes free, is trapped. Roberts chips the puck past the pinching Murzyn, and the speedy Theoren Fleury, reading the play and already in full flight, picks it up in the neutral zone and crosses the Canucks' blue line along the boards. Fleury's winger Robert Reichel lights the afterburner and makes for the other side of the Canucks' net. Lumme somehow manages to stay between them.

When Fleury crosses the line, Canucks goaltender Kirk McLean is well out of the net and committed to him. "Fleury does shoot off the wing a lot," McLean knows. In fact, Fleury had scored the 3–2 go-ahead goal from that side in the second period. "So I was really playing the shooter," McLean was to emphasize later.

But he quickly has doubts. Lumme, staying with the streaking Reichel, is out of his line of sight as McLean squares up toward the left circle. If Lumme isn't there, Fleury is more likely to pass. Lumme is there, but McLean's concern gives him a split-second jump when Fleury decides to pass.

11

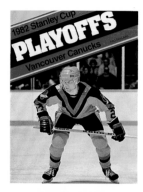

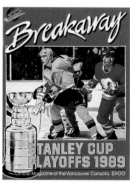

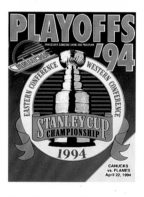

The Calgary–Vancouver rivalry has been a good benchmark of the Canucks' progress. The Flames franchise was built by Cliff Fletcher, who worked for 10 years with the Montreal Canadiens' Sam Pollock. For many years, being in the same division as Calgary (and the great Edmonton clubs) made it difficult for the Canucks to make the playoffs, let alone get very far when they qualified. The 1982 sweep of Calgary was a case of the hottest team in the NHL beating a better club. In 1989 the Canucks again played over their heads, and were unlucky to lose. But the 1994 Canucks were better than the Flames. And luckier.

"Instinct kinda takes over; you're not outthinking yourself or over-compensating."

McLean throws himself feet-first across the goalmouth, just behind the pass, which goes under Lumme's stick. Reichel one-times it. McLean's left pad is on the ice, sweeping forward from underneath after being cocked to launch him across the goal line. The red light goes on, signalling a goal. The puck hits that left toe.

As the bottom pad sweeps forward, it pushes a rebound out and to the right of the net. Canucks left wing Geoff Courtnall is covering Roberts, who is past the rebound before he can react. The puck goes out between Courtnall's feet.

The red goal light is off by now, but Pat Quinn, relieved to be still in the game, vents his displeasure with the goal judge, who is from San Jose. The goal judge nods toward the bench, acknowledging his mistake.

There are several video replays, including a roofbeam shot. "...And with the bottom foot he kicks it out!" raves Jim Peplinski, *Hockey Night in Canada*'s colour man. "His right leg is in behind the goal line," play-by-play man Don Wittman adds, as the puck, in super slo-mo, inches its way toward the net.

If the playoff run that McLean made possible with that save was a long one, the critical stages of the journey that led to it stretched back at least 18 months, to October 1992.

At two consecutive training camps, first at Victoria and then at Kamloops, the coaches had challenged the team to "take the next step." Both years the Canucks came to camp as Smythe Division champions, but as losers of the second round of the playoffs, the division final. The blame could go to Edmonton Oilers goalie Bill Ranford for the 1992 playoff loss. Or maybe the Canucks were just unlucky in 1993 against Los Angeles. But Pat Quinn thinks it was more than that:

"We still hadn't mentally convinced ourselves that we could win in the playoffs. We beat Los Angeles nine out of 11 that season. Yet our team didn't believe it could win that series. And we didn't.

"I thought we were capable of playoff success, from a physical sense, for a couple of years. But we had some learning to do about the more disciplined brand of hockey that can win in the playoffs. What we didn't do was play with the necessary discipline when we lost the puck. We could play the way I like to play, with speed. But our answers in tight situations were risky. Gambling doesn't pay off in this business."

*Until Game 5 of the Calgary series, Vancouver had no power
centre who could match up with the Flames' big Joel Otto.
When Trevor Linden replaced the injured Murray Craven,
that shortcoming no longer existed.*

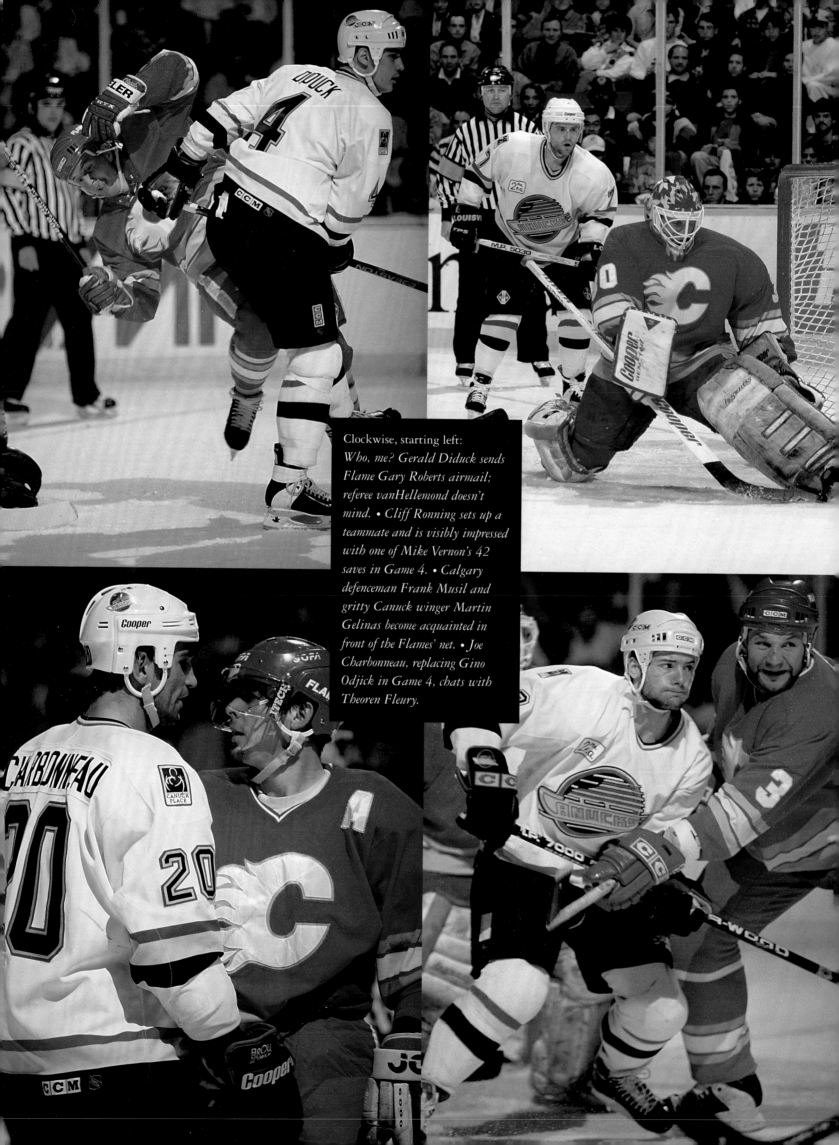

Clockwise, starting left: *Who, me?* Gerald Diduck sends Flame Gary Roberts airmail; referee vanHellemond doesn't mind. • Cliff Ronning sets up a teammate and is visibly impressed with one of Mike Vernon's 42 saves in Game 4. • Calgary defenceman Frank Musil and gritty Canuck winger Martin Gelinas become acquainted in front of the Flames' net. • Joe Charbonneau, replacing Gino Odjick in Game 4, chats with Theoren Fleury.

Designated hitter Shawn Antoski beats the defenceman in an unaccustomed scoring chance, but is foiled by Mike Vernon's neat pokecheck. After his 55-game rookie season, the rugged Antoski looked at home in the playoffs.

Gino Odjick happily pulls Theoren Fleury along for the ride after crossing the Flames' blue line.

An untold story of every playoff season is the good but unlucky player who sits out. Dana Murzyn, the best Canuck defenceman of 1992–93 with a plus-minus of +34, was injured during the Calgary series and did not play again.

Quinn feels that the New York Islanders, after 1976, and the Edmonton Oilers after 1982, had to learn the same lesson. Sometimes the key lessons are the hardest to absorb. "You start to wonder," Quinn remembers, "do we have what it takes, to take the next step?"

At the October 1992 camp in Victoria, Canucks captain Trevor Linden began learning to play centre. Each day he would brief reporters on his painful twice-a-day sessions. As Quinn knew, there were two players who made the difference between the Edmonton Oilers who lost the 1983 Stanley Cup final in four straight to the New York Islanders and the team that won in five the year after. One was Kevin McClelland, a tough centre acquired from Pittsburgh. The other was Incredible Hulk Mark Messier, who moved from left wing to centre. The Canucks needed a Mark Messier-type centre.

The unexpected loss of Anatoli Semenov in the expansion draft and Petr Nedved's decision to test the free-agent market meant that, going into the 1993–94 season, "All of a sudden we weren't so solid" at centre, understates Quinn.

"We moved Trevor in and out and in and out. But I would never force him to play there." When Murray Craven was hurt in Game 4 of the Calgary series, Linden replaced him at centre.

Calgary is a pretty good litmus test for any team's playoff aspirations. "We played them seven times" during the regular schedule, Quinn would remind the team, with Calgary winning four and tieing one. Three of the games were decided by one goal. Calgary's rookie goaltender Trevor Kidd may have made the difference.

"In those seven games the quality of our play didn't get the results. We tried to sell that to the players. We showed them how they were better," Quinn recalled.

Game 1: April 18, 1994. Saddledome, Calgary.

Canucks 5–0. McLean made his playoff commitment obvious with his Game 1 shutout. After the game, Murray Craven told a reporter that over the past few days, the team had seemed a little more composed. "Yesterday at practice we were as focused as I've ever seen. And tonight on the bench we were really focused, too."

Game 2: April 20, 1994. Saddledome, Calgary.

Flames 7–5. Gary Roberts became the Flames' irresistible force, running McLean twice and earning himself the title "Public Enemy No.1" in Vancouver.

Game 3: April 22, 1994. Pacific Coliseum, Vancouver.

Flames 4–2. The next two games in Vancouver could have gone either way; this one was a scoreless tie after two periods.

Geoff Courtnall, after his overtime Gretzky-imitation slapshot wins Game 5, jumps for joy on Pavel Bure.

Bure-hug: Double-overtime seventh-game winner Pavel Bure is hugged by Dave Babych and Greg Adams before the rest of the Canucks arrive to celebrate their third straight overtime victory over Calgary.

Game 4: April 24, 1994. Pacific Coliseum, Vancouver.

Flames 3–2. Vernon, getting hotter as the series progressed, stole the game with a 42-save performance to give the Flames a 3–1 stranglehold on the series.

The Canucks still were not getting the results against Calgary. Were they unlucky again? Assistant coach Ron Smith thought so.

Game 5: April 26, 1994. Saddledome, Calgary.

Canucks 2–1. Part of winning hockey games is refusing to allow luck to play a role, and not getting into situations where accidents can happen. The raw truth for the Canucks that evening was that they had to take destiny into their own hands or be broken up over the summer.

Even down three games to one, "I remember saying to Pat, 'We should beat this team,'" Smith says. "We decided to challenge the team, not let them off the hook.

"It was an easy call in some ways. The year before, the team hadn't been prodded against L.A. There was a feeling among the players [that if they didn't win] there would be changes. There had been a lot of patience here, a lot of tolerance toward people. That was a little bit of a message to the players. That message was delivered."

What a reply. Regulation time ended 1–1 with Pavel Bure scoring his first of the series, and then a telegraph wired over Vernon's glove and into the top left corner in overtime. The message: Even the hottest netminder can be beaten, kindest regards, Geoff Courtnall. Canucks 2–1. Lesson learned.

Game 6: April 28, 1994. Pacific Coliseum, Vancouver.

Canucks 3–2. The word "miracle" began to creep into the newspaper coverage after Calgary took a penalty for too many men in overtime. Quinn called a timeout. Just get the shot on the net, he told his power play. Linden won the draw, Bure got the shot on the net (although it hit Jyrki Lumme) and the puck found its way to the tape on Linden's stick. He scooped it in.

Game 7: April 30, 1994. Saddledome, Calgary.

Canucks 4–3. With the seconds in regulation ticking away, Smith wondered what was going on. The Canucks were losing 3–2. Although they were in Calgary's zone, "We were doing nothing.

"It was the same feeling everybody had when we were losing the earlier games. We were giving up some chances. McLean made a great save – was it on German Titov? – probably just as tough as the save on Reichel. I remember thinking, why are we doing nothing?"

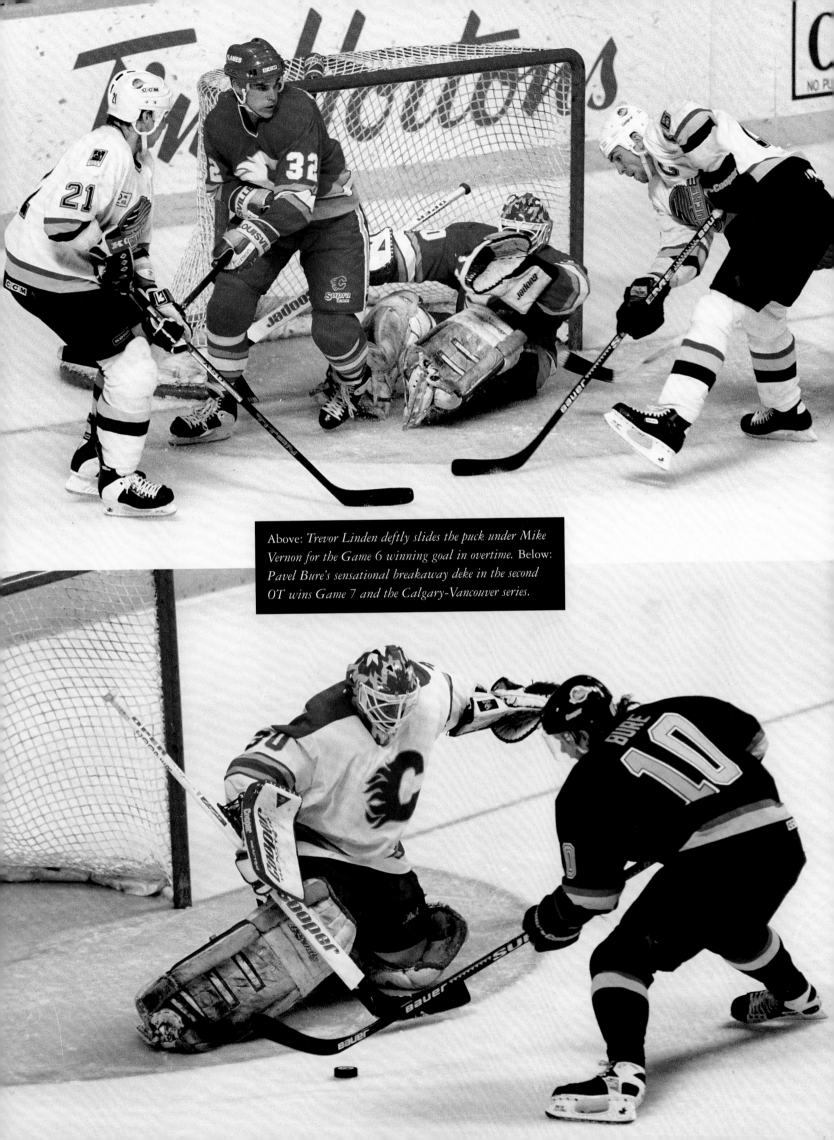

Above: *Trevor Linden deftly slides the puck under Mike Vernon for the Game 6 winning goal in overtime.* Below: *Pavel Bure's sensational breakaway deke in the second OT wins Game 7 and the Calgary-Vancouver series.*

Clockwise, starting left: *Cliff Ronning has his hands full with Dallas sniper Mike Modano.* • *Kirk McLean turns aside Russ Courtnall's blast while blanking Dallas 3–0 in Game 2.* • *Nathan LaFayette eyes Modano as Murray Craven anticipates a drop pass.* • *Dave Babych has leverage on Dallas's Pelle Eklund.*

Coliseum fans register awe as Pavel Bure scores his second breakaway goal of Game 5, the goal that puts the Stars on ice 4–1 and gives him his second two-goal game of the series. After his second straight 60-goal season, Bure started slowly in the playoffs. By the Dallas series, the Rocket was in a higher orbit.

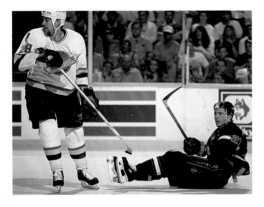

Replacing the injured Dana Murzyn, Brian Glynn flattens hardrock Star Shane Churla.

And then Greg Adams, who always seems to appear at the last moment out of nowhere, scooped up a loose puck in Calgary's left corner, walked in front, and lifted a backhand that hit Vernon's pads, fell behind him, and grew little feet to stagger somehow over the Calgary goal line. It was 3–3. Overtime.

This was the miracle for Ron Smith, a link between the Canucks' two runs to the Stanley Cup final and a man who knows a higher force at work when he sees one. This was Smith's '94 equivalent of Colin Campbell's two goals in one game during the '82 run.

Kirk McLean is still busily keeping possibilities alive in the Game 7 second overtime. He neatly deflects Wes Walz's centring pass directly in front, to Jyrki Lumme. Moments later, he hits Linden at the left boards with a pass after fielding Walz's long shot, and Linden sends Adams into the Calgary Zone, where he gets dumped....

It is three shifts or so into the second overtime. The exact time cannot be pinpointed because there are so few stoppages in playoff hockey. There's no time to check the clock. But at the end of his shift, Martin Gelinas brakes just short of the Calgary blue line and dumps the puck into their zone. This starts the critical sequence of events. The Canucks change on the fly.

Gelinas' shootaround comes along the boards to Paul Kruse, who chips it hard out of the zone. The puck slides to Dave Babych, the Canucks' left defenceman, who takes it on his forehand and, in one sweep, backhands the puck along his own blue line to his partner, Jeff Brown.

Brown seems to gather the puck in to himself, pauses to look down at it as if conferring some special power on the disc, looks up, and sees Pavel Bure breaking out of a cluster of players at the Calgary blue line. The pass is six inches off the ice, through the knot of players, and on Bure's stick. He has a step on everybody else.

McLean has a good view of the play. Brown and Bure had hooked up the same way during the first period, but Bure lost control of the puck. "This time," McLean says, "I was praying."

"I thought the pass was for me," Trevor Linden says later. "Thank God Pavel got it and not me. He went right under me and across the blue line. I had a great view of the goal."

Calgary defenceman Zarley Zalapski turns and hooks Bure several times, but overextends himself and falls.

Linesman Dan Schachte escorts Sergio Momesso from the ice after he is called for interference by referee Don Koharski. Momesso offers some heartfelt advice.

John McIntyre holds up Toronto's Doug Gilmour, who, Sun *columnist Denny Boyd writes, "has the face of a refugee in a war-zone newsreel."*

Tim Hunter slows down Wendel Clark's pursuit of the puck.

Bure fakes quickly to his backhand, comes back to his forehand, and waits for Mike Vernon to fully extend himself. Real snipers never rush the moment of truth.

Then he taps it through the few inches left between Vernon's pad and the goalpost. Zalapski follows the puck into the Calgary goal, taking Vernon with him.

"That was an outstanding series," Pat Quinn would say afterward. "I've said this many times: We could've not won that series and I'd still have been satisfied with how we played. If we'd have lost it I'd still have been proud of how we played."

For Ron Smith, the Dallas and Toronto series held few surprises. The Stars won the middle game of the five-game set, but, on the whole, it was "a pretty workmanlike execution of a team by another team playing at the top of its game, giving the other team nothing."

Nonetheless, it will be remembered as the series when Pavel Bure ceased being Don Cherry's little weasel and became a complete Canadian hockey player. Hit from behind by Dallas defenceman Derian Hatcher in a corner scrum during Game 2, Bure rocketed back after the play to level Shane Churla near the Canucks net, knocking the Dallas hardrock into the middle of the next period. The league fined Bure $500 for an offence that went officially unnoticed during the game, prompting an enterprising radio station to organize the Pavel Bure Defence Fund. The proceeds, twice Bure's fine, went to Canuck Place, the Shaughnessy hospice for terminally ill children. The fuss did not quite obscure the fact that Bure struck for two goals in the game, his best game so far, Linden thought.

"He scored like always," the Canucks captain told Archie McDonald of *The Vancouver Sun*. "But he was smart. He didn't take penalties."

For many, though, winning the series with the Maple Leafs was the highlight of the entire playoff run. Afterward, *The Sun*'s "Pride of Vancouver" souvenir pullout section was headlined: "Life is still good. After all, we beat Toronto."

Smith had analysed tape of both teams. While Toronto's Game 1 win in Toronto on May 16 came as a surprise, Smith told a friend immediately after the game that he expected the Canucks to win the next four straight. The Leafs' Game 1 overtime win was as good as things would get for them.

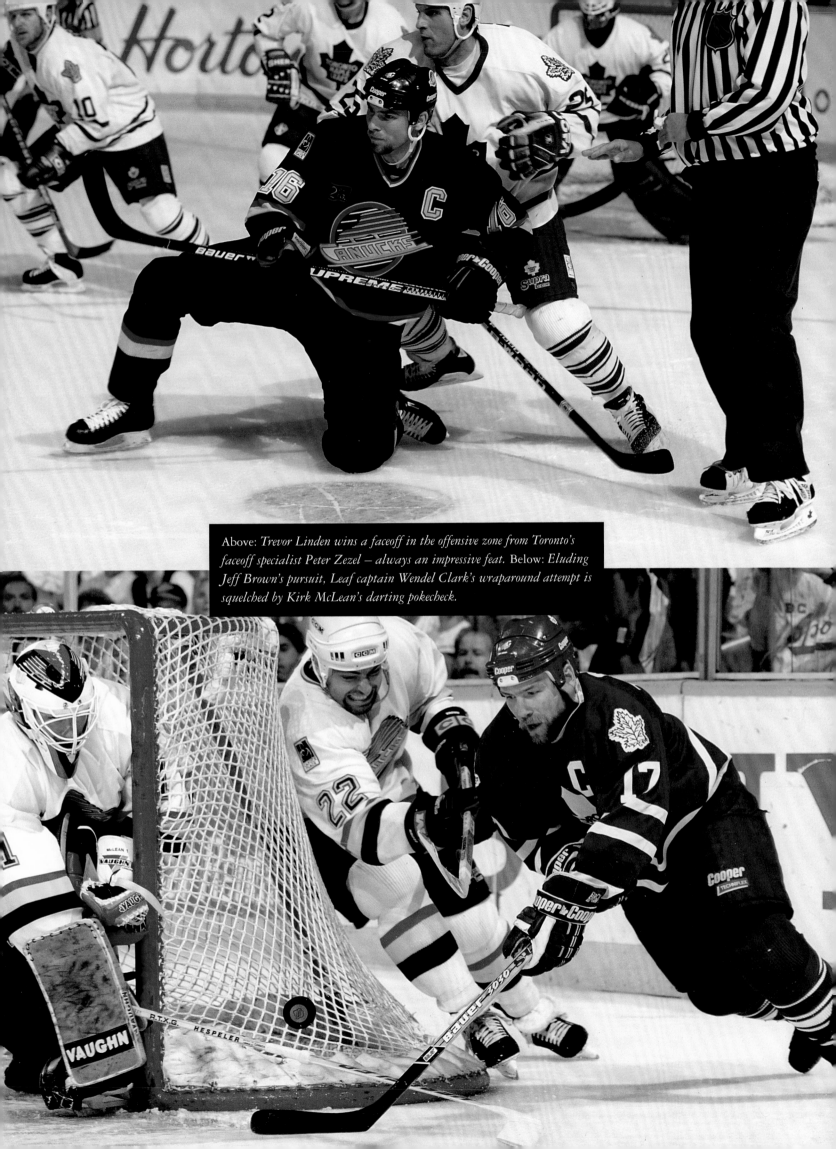

Above: *Trevor Linden wins a faceoff in the offensive zone from Toronto's faceoff specialist Peter Zezel — always an impressive feat.* Below: *Eluding Jeff Brown's pursuit, Leaf captain Wendel Clark's wraparound attempt is squelched by Kirk McLean's darting pokecheck.*

Above: *Murray Craven's wraparound attempt has Geoff Courtnall (in the corner) ready to celebrate.* Below: *When the rejoicing begins at 10:01 pm PST, May 24, 1994, after another Greg Adams overtime score to eliminate the Leafs, everybody's in on it.*

Captain Trevor Linden carries the Clarence S. Campbell Bowl to centre ice at the Coliseum after the 4–3 double-overtime win over Toronto.

Amidst the jubilation, Canucks owner Arthur Griffiths congratulates Greg Adams on yet another timely score. This one finished the Leafs.

Mrs. Emily Griffiths, widow of Hall-of-Famer Frank Griffiths, celebrates the moment with Trevor Linden.

"The true picture was that there was no way we should lose to those teams, assuming we played our game. We grind you, we grind you, we grind you, and then our big player beats you. Like the Islanders used to. Everybody played their role."

For Kirk McLean, as for so many others, the entire series against Toronto was a highlight. It was more a case of playing well in Maple Leaf Gardens, a building where Captain Kirk doesn't feel he has been impressive. But he is not especially proud of his back-to-back shutouts against the Leafs. Was he playing at his best? "I don't think so."

He was saving his best for last. A timely goal from Gus Adams in double overtime finished the Leafs. The Canucks' playoff record after April 26 and Game 5 of the Calgary series was 11–2.

The Canucks had come this far in the playoffs before. And, while this 1994 Vancouver team was bigger and more talented than the storied 1982 club, making the Stanley Cup final was more of a surprise in 1994. Especially for the coaches.

The 1982 team "had been playing tight, tough, smart hockey for some time," recalls Ron Smith, an assistant with both the 1982 and 1994 teams. "In some ways, it was more expected, by far, that time. This year, there was every reason not to have high expectations. There was no real indicator."

Shortly before he retired, Canucks all-star centre Thomas Gradin brought a European frame of reference to his thoughts about the development of the hockey club he contributed to for seven years. Gradin saw the franchise as a kind of North American cathedral, and he hoped that he and the other players of his early-80s vintage had added a row of stones to part of the wall. In fact, Stan Smyl believes, Gradin never got the credit he deserved for the consistency of craftsmanship he displayed: "You knew how he was going to play every night," Steamer says.

Distinguished contributions like those of Stan Smyl and Thomas Gradin – both still with the club, by the way – become cults with losing teams. Winners celebrate those who have gone before and, as the winning continues, those from whose hands the torch is passed stay with us as heroes.

There are now 24 years' worth of heroes to celebrate, beginning with the rejects of the dozen existing teams who made up the original NHL Vancouver Canucks. These were the guys who laid the foundations.

NATIONAL HOCKEY LEAGUE

OFFICIAL REPORT OF MATCH

* STARTERS

\#1

Vancouver vs. Los Angeles   Oct. 9, 1970

Played in ... Vancouver

Rink, Date.

	HOME CLUB		Y or N				VISITING CLUB		Y or N
No.			Y	Goal *	No.	30	DEJORDY		N
30	GARDNER		N	Sub-Goal	1	NORRIS		Y
* 1	HODGE	"A"	Y	Defence	2	HOGANSON		Y
2	DOAK		Y	"	3	CAHAN		Y
3	QUINN		Y	" *	4	MAROTTE	"A"	Y
4	WILKENS		Y	"	5	PRICE	"A"	Y
* 5	SLY		Y	" *	21	RAVLICH		
* 6	REAUME			"				
19	TALLON			"	7	DUFF		N
				Forward	8	LONSBERRY		Y
* 7	BOUDRIAS		Y	" *	9	LABOSSIERE		Y
8	JOHNSON	"A"	Y	"	11	ROBINSON		Y
10	CULLEN		Y	"	12	MICKEY		Y
11	MAKI		Y	"	15	WIDING		Y
12	CORRIGAN		Y	"	16	JOYAL		Y
* 18	PAIEMENT		Y	"	17	FLETT		Y
18	POPIEL		Y	" *	18	BERRY		Y
* 23	HALL		Y	"	20	PULFORD	"A"	Y
24	LUNDE		Y	" *	24	BYERS		
25	KURTENBACH	"C"	Y					

Game starting time 8.22 P.M. First period ended at 8.58 P.M. Second period
started at 9.21 P.M. and ended at 9.54 P.M. Third period started at 10.11
P.M. and ended at 10.53 P.M.   Score 3 to 1

Won by ... Los Angeles   Game Timekeeper CAL PILKEY

Official Scorer KEN STEIN

Penalty Timekeeper SYD MORREY

Goal Judges J. McGOWAN, S. McGOWAN

Linesmen N. ARMSTRONG, M. ASHFORD

REMARKS:

Signed ... _____ Referee

_____ Official-Scorer

SPECIAL INSTRUCTIONS

... in the appropriate column all players who *actually* played in the game and indicate those who did not actually play with
... essential information.
... than fifteen minutes after the advertised time should be reported, stating the cause of the delay and the club at fault
... ecting the conduct of the game should also be reported.
... dispatched to National Hockey League, 922 Sun Life Building, by the quickest possible means.

Official NHL scoresheet from the Vancouver Canucks' first game, October 9, 1970, and the puck defenceman Barry Wilkins used to score the club's first goal.

Two years after the Vancouver Millionaires won the Stanley Cup — then a challenge cup — the NHL was formed, November 22, 1917. The ups and downs of the Jazz Age, the Depression and World War II drained professional hockey. Not until 1967 did the NHL orchestrate a successful expansion plan — from six to 12 teams, setting the stage for the Vancouver Canucks' big-league hockey debut in 1970.

Black Tuesday

News cameras recorded this "Wheel of Fortune" in action as it determined the drafting positions of the NHL's new 1970–71 teams, the Vancouver Canucks and the Buffalo Sabres.

Canucks draft table, June 11, 1970. Clockwise from left: Walter "Babe" Pratt; unidentified; western scout Phil Maloney (obscured); Ontario scout Jack MacDonald; coach Hal Laycoe; John "Peanuts" O'Flaherty; eastern scout Vern Buffey; GM and vice-president Norman "Bud" Poile; Greg Douglas (right foreground).

Facing page: *Orland Kurtenbach won dignity with his fists and penalty-killing in the six-team NHL. Centre on New York Ranger teams that had Jean Ratelle and Walt Tkaczuk at that critical position, he was the Canucks' "Captain Kurt" until 1974.*

JUNE 9, 1970: GRAND SALON, QUEEN ELIZABETH HOTEL, MONTREAL. There was something carnival-like, right from the beginning, about using a "Wheel of Fortune" to determine which of the two new clubs would draft Gilbert Perreault. It was costing the Vancouver Canucks and the Buffalo Sabres $6 million each – three times what the 1967 expansion teams had paid – to join the National Hockey League. "Far too much," in Buffalo GM-coach Punch Imlach's opinion, "for getting the leavings of the other clubs in the league." They deserved better.

The wheel-spinning was an attempt to inject drama into an already melodramatic event. Buffalo co-owner Seymour Knox had lobbied the league, at Imlach's request, to know the order of the drafting in advance of the amateur draft itself – by two days if possible – to allow time to consider his options. "I wanted Perreault as I had never wanted a hockey player before," Imlach acknowledged in his memoir, *Heaven and Hell in the NHL*. "The hair just stood up on my neck at what he could do."

The room was jammed; everybody in hockey was there. Vancouver's drafting contingent included Vice-President and General Manager Bud Poile and Head Coach Hal Laycoe. NHL president Clarence Campbell was presiding and was set to spin the wheel, which would determine the order of selection in the expansion draft the next day, and then the amateur draft two days later. The wheel was numbered one to 12. Imlach and Poile tossed a coin to see who would pick the numbers for both spins. Imlach won and chose the high numbers.

In the first spin, Imlach won when the wheel stopped at eight. Buffalo would choose first in the expansion draft.

You could have heard a pin drop in the crowded ballroom as Campbell spun the wheel for a second time. When it finally came to rest, the league president shouted: "Number one! Vancouver wins first choice in the amateur draft!" Whoops of joy went up from a jubilant Canuck table.

But Imlach was on his feet, and so was the rest of the Sabres' table, pointing and yelling, "Eleven! Eleven!"

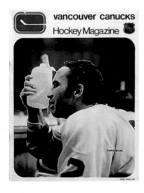

First-year Canuck programs.
Top: *For assistant captain Gary Doak, 18 months with the Canucks was preferable to 44 games at the end of the bench with Boston's 1969–70 Stanley Cup winners.* Centre: *Wayne Maki joined Orland Kurtenbach and Murray Hall on the club's first line, scoring six goals in the first eight games and 25 for the season.* Bottom: *Two-time Vezina Trophy winner Charlie Hodge, drafted from Montreal, had a winning record and nifty 3.41 GAA as one of several former WHL Canucks with the NHL team.*

Campbell took another look. The digits in the double figures were one above the other. He agreed, "There has been a mistake. The winning number is 11...."

It was time for the Sabres' table to erupt with joy, even as the smiles at the Canucks' table had yet to fade. Imlach smiled, sat down, and theatrically wiped his brow to the exaggerated laughter of all around him. Two days later he selected Perreault. Imlach awarded his new star jersey number 11, Buffalo's lucky number on the "Wheel of Fortune," which he wore for his entire 17-year career with the Sabres. Perreault broke a 45-year record for goals by a rookie in 1970–71 with 38.

The Canucks, having regained their composure, chose Dale Tallon, a promising 19-year-old from the Toronto Marlboros of the Ontario Hockey Association, who could play either forward or defence. Tallon had 45 assists his first year in the NHL, despite his yearnings for a career in professional golf. Hindsight tells us that Reg Leach, Rick MacLeish or Darryl Sittler might have been a better choice as the new team's first franchise player. Then again, maybe not.

That original Canucks team was assembled by Hall of Famer (builder category) Bud Poile, the architect of the first Philadelphia Flyers team three years before. Vancouver drafted astutely in the dispersal draft of players from the established clubs: Gary Doak, Bobby Orr's once and future defence partner; centre and captain Orland Kurtenbach, rookie of the year with the Western Hockey League Canucks in 1957–58; and Rosaire Paiement, penalty-minute leader in the American League the year before, who would score 34 goals for the Canucks during their inaugural season. Defenceman Barry Wilkins was drafted from Boston, and soon took a permanent place of honour in Vancouver franchise history with the first goal – assist, Len Lunde – scored at 2:14 of the third period of a 3–1 loss to the Los Angeles Kings, October 9, 1970. Andre Boudrias was sold to the Canucks by St. Louis on expansion draft day, and went on to average 27 goals his first three seasons and set an all-time club record with 62 assists in 1974–75. He is still 11th in career goals (passed last year by Pavel Bure) and fourth in assists on the all-time Canuck list.

Their fourth pick was John Brian Patrick Quinn, a six-foot-three 215-pound defenceman from the Toronto Maple Leafs. Quinn, 26, too young for the outgoing Imlach regime and too old for new Leaf GM Jim Gregory's youth movement, extended a career that would bring him back to Vancouver in 1987 to make the Canucks Stanley Cup contenders. Quinn was happy to be drafted.

Barry Wilkins' first-ever Canucks goal was scored on Los Angeles goaltender Denis DeJordy at 2:14 of the third period of the Canuck first NHL game, a 3–1 loss to the Kings. Andre Boudrias, number 7 is checked by the Kings' Dale Hoganson, while Len Lunde, number 24, who assisted on the goal with a pass at the Kings blue line, is tied up by Juha Widing.

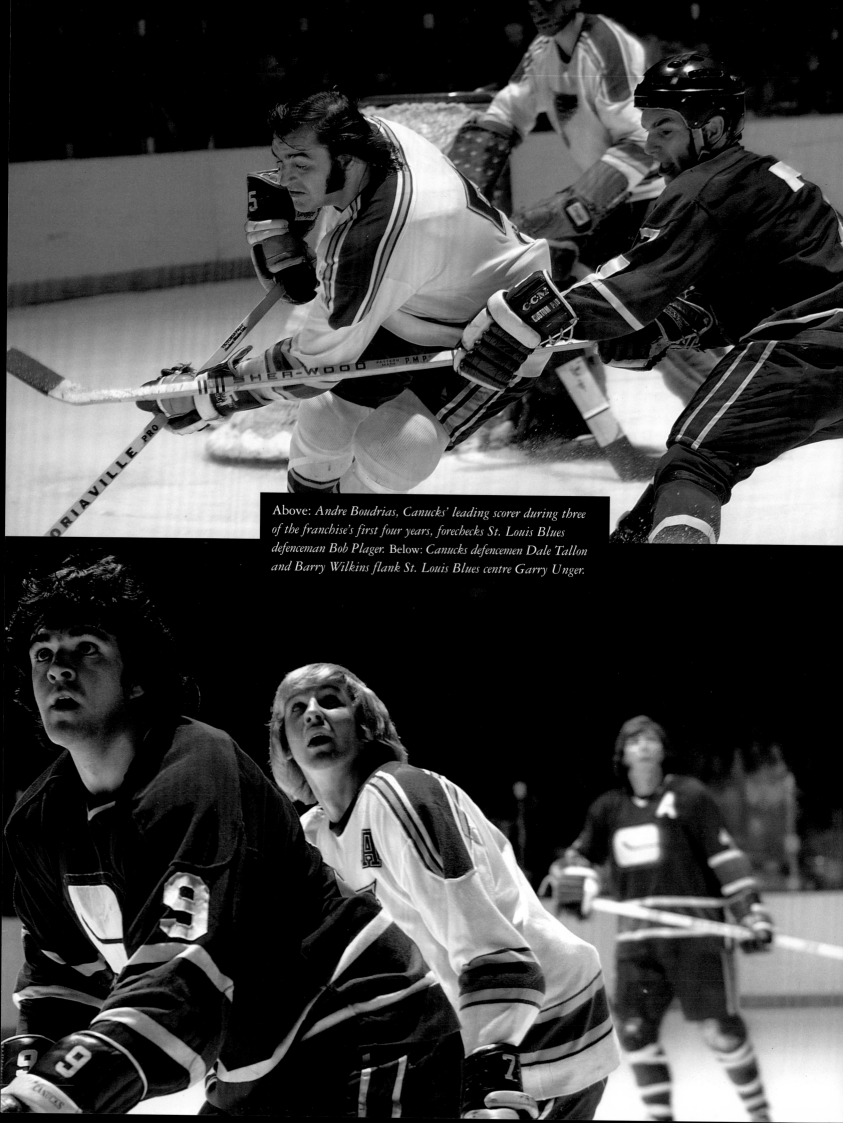

Above: *Andre Boudrias, Canucks' leading scorer during three of the franchise's first four years, forechecks St. Louis Blues defenceman Bob Plager.* Below: *Canucks defencemen Dale Tallon and Barry Wilkins flank St. Louis Blues centre Garry Unger.*

PAT QUINN   DEFENSE

VANCOUVER CANUCKS

MURRAY HALL   CENTER

VANCOUVER CANUCKS

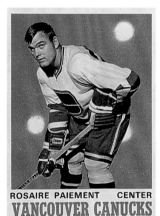

ROSAIRE PAIEMENT   CENTER

VANCOUVER CANUCKS

O-Pee-Chee shares its wisdom about this trio of Canucks on the flip side of these collector cards. Top: "A hard-hitting defenceman, Pat is at his best when the opposition attempts to rough it up a bit and will give the Canucks a defenceman that will keep opposing forwards on their toes." Centre: "A veteran in the minor pro leagues, Murray has played 55 games in the NHL in the past nine seasons, and like Orland Kurtenbach, will give the Canucks experience at centre ice – played for Vancouver the last two seasons in the WHL. Bottom: "Rosaire could be the 'policeman' Vancouver needs in its first season in the NHL. He loves the rough going and will not back down from the NHL's 'tough guys.'"

"Actually, I liked the team. It was a good group of journeyman-type guys. Our goaltending was good. It was a talented, interesting bunch. We had a full audience of quiet people who were still Maple Leaf fans."

They did better than expected. Paiement scored 34 goals and sat through 154 penalty minutes, leading the team in both categories. Andre Boudrias led the team in points, as he would three of the club's first four years. Coach Laycoe would long remember how goaltender Charlie Hodge, who had played only 12 games in each of the preceding two seasons with Montreal, won 15, lost 13 and tied five — a winning record with an expansion team. The Canucks went 24–46–8 under Laycoe, good for sixth in the East Division. It was a record that subsequent Canuck editions were unable to improve upon for four years. They regressed in 1971–72, dropping eight points and finishing seventh.

"Human nature took over" during the franchise's second year, Quinn thinks. "Some guys sat down, put their feet up, and said 'I'm a National Leaguer.'"

For Quinn, the Canucks offered a chance to play regularly and develop. Of all the original NHL Canucks drafted from other teams, Quinn lasted the longest in the league – six more years (long enough to accumulate 950 NHL penalty minutes), five with the Atlanta Flames after being picked in the next (1972) expansion draft. He was always in demand. He was the second captain in Flames history and went directly from playing to coaching.

Several developments during 1973–74 ended the Canucks' initial honeymoon era. General manager Bud Poile fell ill and handed his office to Hal Laycoe, who then appointed Bill McCreary to replace him behind the bench in time for the 1973 season.

The real power in the club's executive suite, however, was hotelier Coley Hall, a shareholder in the minor-league team who operated the Canucks on behalf of Medicor, Inc., of Minneapolis, owners of the Ice Follies. Hall was the recipient of much free advice on how an NHL franchise should be run, and he took too much of it. Too often the advice was to fire the coach.

McCreary was the third coach in the four-year history of the team, following Laycoe and Vic Stasiuk, and he lasted until mid-January 1974. Hall phoned Phil Maloney, a three-team NHL player and a star with the WHL Canucks, then happily coaching the Canucks' Seattle Totems farm club. Maloney knew better than to refuse the offer.

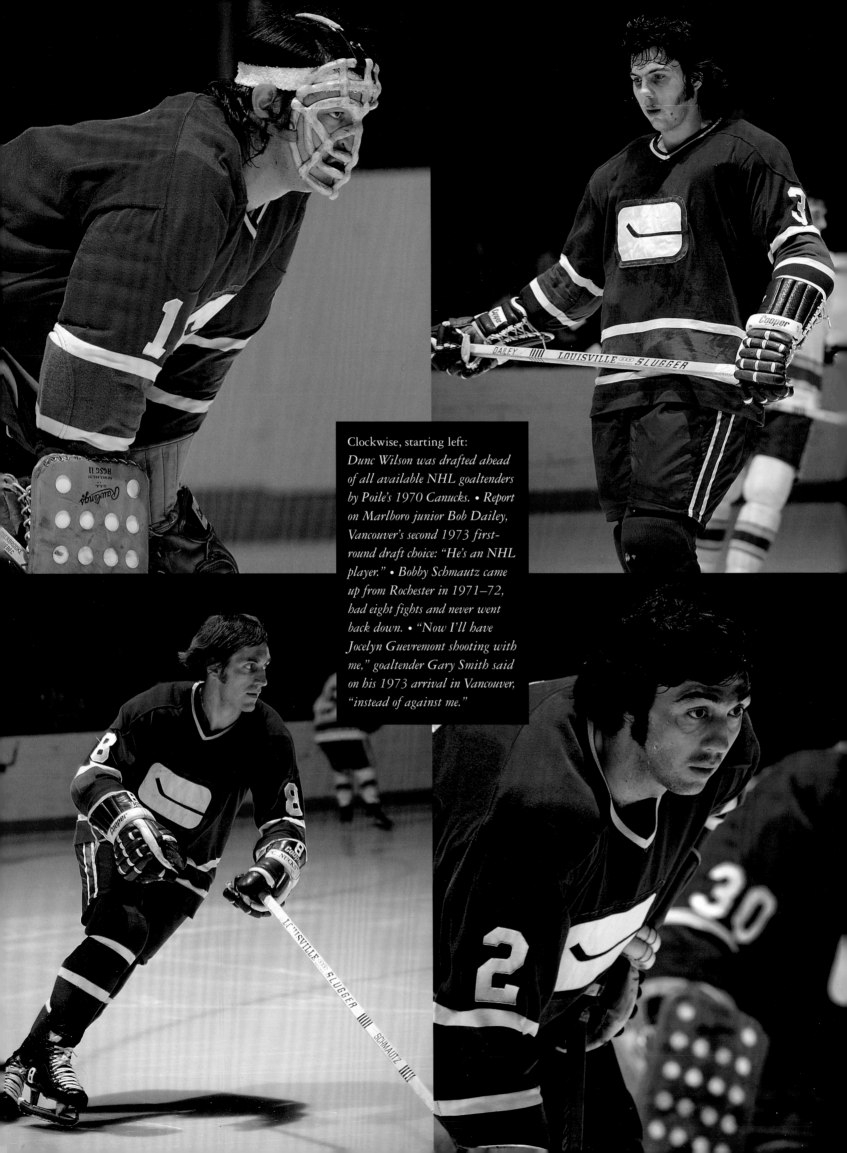

Clockwise, starting left: *Dunc Wilson was drafted ahead of all available NHL goaltenders by Poile's 1970 Canucks.* • *Report on Marlboro junior Bob Dailey, Vancouver's second 1973 first-round draft choice: "He's an NHL player."* • *Bobby Schmautz came up from Rochester in 1971–72, had eight fights and never went back down.* • *"Now I'll have Jocelyn Guevremont shooting with me," goaltender Gary Smith said on his 1973 arrival in Vancouver, "instead of against me."*

DALE TALLON'S TRUE VALUE

It was inevitable that Dale Tallon would disappoint. As the Canucks' equivalent to Buffalo's Gilbert Perreault as a franchise-founding draft choice, Tallon would always suffer in comparison. By 1975 Perreault and the Sabres had made the Stanley Cup final, losing honorably to Philadelphia's second consecutive Cup-winning team.

By then Tallon was two years gone from Vancouver. Tallon was a consensus second pick in the 1970–71 draft, so choosing him was not necessarily a mistake. In his three years with the Canucks, his overall point totals dropped as he became more of a two-way defenceman. He did score 62 points for Chicago in 1975–76.

But nothing he did in Vancouver became Dale Tallon as much as his leaving in May 1973. By then he had played for four coaches. He was traded for Jerry Korab, an eventual 15-year NHL defenceman (mainly with Buffalo), who brought John Gould and Tracy Pratt in trade later that year. With Korab came Gary Smith.

Tallon was traded for three key players in the Canucks' 1974–75 divisional championship season. No first-round draft choice would prove to be as valuable on the open market until Garth Butcher (1981) or Petr Nedved (1990). Which of those two brought more value to the Canucks? Good question.

Seventeen days later, the reluctant coach was also general manager. In the remaining 37 games of the 1973–74 season, Maloney turned McCreary's 9–25–7 (.304) Canucks into a .460 club. His first acquisition was Chris Oddleifson, a 13-goal scorer with Boston for whom Maloney gave up popular hustling winger Bobby Schmautz, a 38-goal scorer in 1972–73.

During the summer of 1974, Medicor sold the Canucks to the late Frank Griffiths' Western Broadcasting Co. for $9 million. No sooner had the Griffiths family assumed control than competition appeared in the form of the WHA's Miami Screaming Eagles/Philadelphia Blazers franchise, which moved to Vancouver and took up offices in the southeast corner of the Coliseum, opposite the Canucks' quarters on the Renfrew Street side.

The Blazers' coaching staff had deep roots in Vancouver: Joe Crozier had been a shareholder in the WHL Canucks and their last coach. He had expected to coach the NHL Canucks. Andy Bathgate, Crozier's assistant, had finished his great career with the Canucks, the top New York Rangers farm club. The Blazers hired longtime radio personality and columnist Denny Boyd as their publicist and began making inroads into the Vancouver hockey market.

From all this turmoil emerged the Canucks' first divisional championship.

Following pages: *George "It's time I got serious" Gardner, 29 years old during the 1971–72 season, looks for a shot from the Black Hawks' left point. Barry Wilkins leans on Stan Mikita and John Schella stands guard. Gardner's GAA in 24 games that year was 4.17.*

The Canucks joined the league with the colours of west coast cool: blue, green and white. The new colours of 1978 were "hot and aggressive."

Seven years after expansion, the NHL experienced a breakthrough. The 1973–74 Philadelphia Flyers became the first expansion team to claim Lord Stanley's mug, an indication of the future, as expansion teams would win 13 of the next 20 Stanley Cup finals. In the wake of the Flyers' victory, the 1974–75 Vancouver Canucks built a team that fashioned a season worth remembering and savouring.

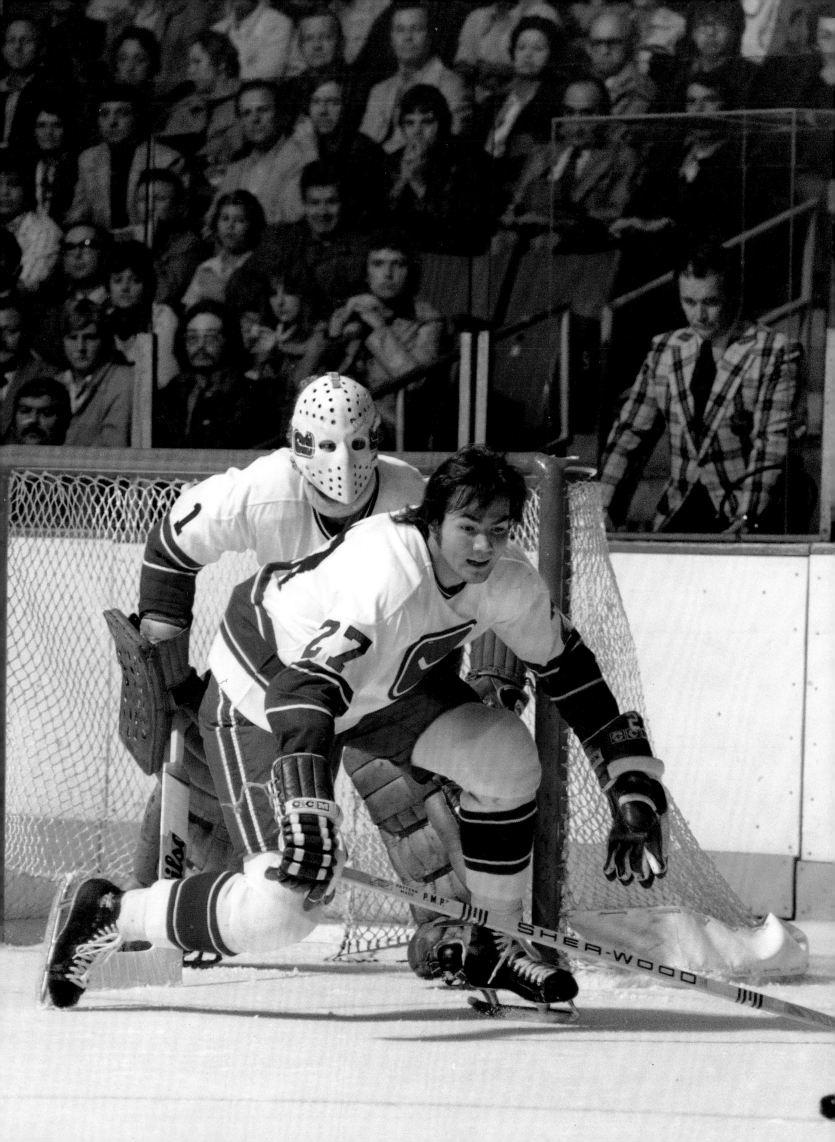

Building a Contender

The late Frank Griffiths loved life and all its possibilities. The same competitive zeal that built a broadcasting empire went into making the Canucks competitive. In his first year as owner, the Canucks won their first division championship.

Phil Maloney, who could quote Freud or build a house, became an NHL coach and GM in three weeks early in 1973. His assessment of the 1974–75 team: "I should sit up and pound the table and say we're going to finish first," he said. "But I've got to be realistic."

Facing page: *Harold Snepsts, the all-time fan favourite, blocks a shot for Gary Smith, the most colourful Canuck ever.*

FEBRUARY 14, 1975. PACIFIC COLISEUM.

It happened in the last minute of the game, Canucks 5, Red Wings 4. An inept effort for both teams had steadily degenerated into a late-third-period brawl. Referee Ron Wicks had excused four Canucks from further play, leaving the team two men short on the ice. Goaltender Gary Smith, who had been the loser in a run-in with Wicks not long before, figured the referee owed him one.

And so it was that when the Wings skated into the Canucks' zone on a 3-on-1 break, Pierre Jarry took a pass at the top of the circle to Smith's left and one-timed it to Smith's short side. The goalie did not catch the puck because his catching mitt was gripping the left post and pulling it upward.

Lifting the net off its four-inch anchor pin in those days took real strength, a strength belied by Smith's sense of humour and radiant smile, and the Shirley Temple blond curls that popped out from under Smith's mask. But he did it.

And as the puck entered the dislodged net and the red light flashed, "Wicks didn't hesitate," Smith says now. "He just blew the whistle and signalled for a faceoff."

No goal. The Canucks took the two points by which they beat St. Louis for first place in the division, and banked one of the six wins by which they exceeded the .500 break-even mark in 1974–75, the first Canuck team to do so.

Everything had to go right for the Canucks to be division-championship contenders for the first time ever. Astute coaching, brilliant goaltending, some career years from the forwards and a little luck on the road were important factors in the Canucks' first division championship – and their last for seven years.

"People forget," says the coach and GM of that team, Phil Maloney, "the Vancouver Blazers were in town. I thought it was a crucial year for us. We had to do well. It might have been us going off to Calgary" – as the Blazers did – "after the season."

ONE OF A KIND
With Gary "Suitcase" Smith, the goaltender who joined the Canucks and played 66 games in 1973–74, the Canucks moved into a whole new dimension.

Smith had style. He wore a full-length lynx coat during the season. He was part of the *Hockey Night In Canada* opening montage – the big goalie, in Oakland Seals yellow, stickhandling past his own blue line in an effort to be the first netminder to score. His other unrealized ambition was to punt the puck over the scoreboard in Maple Leaf Gardens; he did get it out of his zone. Between periods he had a ritual: He stripped off all his equipment and put it back on just to keep himself occupied.

Nobody gets away with that stuff without delivering. Smith had shared a Vezina Trophy with Tony Esposito at his last place of business, the Chicago Black Hawks. The Canucks traded their original franchise player, Dale Tallon, to get him. With the Canucks in 1974–75, he had the greatest season of any Canuck goalie – among several great seasons – until Kirk McLean.

At his introduction to the Vancouver media in August 1973 by then-coach Hal Laycoe, Smith had the wit to reply "I just want to say Hal told you the truth. I *am* a great goaltender and a great team man."

Smith was that rare sociable goalie who organized beer at the Coachhouse Inn after practices and was always in the middle of celebrations. His nocturnal habits didn't seem to affect his on-ice performances. His six shutouts are still the team record for a season, while his 72 games with a GAPG of 3.09 was the best year any first-string Canuck goalie had until Kirk McLean's 2.74 in 1991–92.

Smith's lifetime season did not go unnoticed around the league. He finished fifth in Hart Trophy balloting, highest of any Canuck until Pavel Bure.

Gary Smith rose to the occasion. So much did the goaltender personify the Canucks' organization in 1974–75 that Fred Shero, on his way to a second straight Stanley Cup with the Flyers, called them a one-man team.

But no player knows better than the goaltender that hockey is a team game. Smith credits the rest of the team, starting at the top.

"Phil Maloney was the first coach I played for who was a good guy," Smith remembers, "and so the pressure was off."

Maloney remembers Bill McCreary's edicts: "They'd had to wear ties and jackets and keep their hair cut, so the first thing I told them is 'I don't care if your hair is down to your waists and you wear dresses as long as you stay out of jail and show up on time for the games.' I didn't really mean they could wear dresses," Maloney chuckles. It was 1973, man.

"So that was right up my alley," Smith says.

Maloney had coached 37 games the previous season after replacing McCreary. In 1974–75 the Canucks opened up a 23-point lead in the division before Christmas.

"Looking back on it," Smith says now, "we had a real good start. Eight of 10? Something like that. We were barely a .500 team from then on."

Smith's defence consisted mostly of rookies and newcomers, and a few seasoned pros. Tracy Pratt, Smith believes, had "a great year," playing 79 games, more than he played in any year of his long pro career. Smith liked Dennis Kearns even though Kearns was out of favour with the fans at the time for not being a hitter; every goalie likes defencemen who can move the puck.

Otherwise, it was a revamped blueline corps, all the more remarkable for their outstanding season. In his rookie year, Big Bob Dailey scored 48 points. Harold Snepsts brought his size and likability to the team in mid-season. Two useful defenders, John Grisdale and Mike Robitaille, joined the Canucks that year in trades.

The Canucks finished eighth in team scoring that year, higher than they had any business rising, but not so high that Smith ever had much of a lead to work with. In his third season, Don Lever scored 38 goals. Newcomer John Gould had 34, Gerry O'Flaherty had 25, and Andre Boudrias put 62 assists with his 16 goals to lead the team in points with 78. Dennis Ververgaert, Leon Rochefort, the exciting Bobby Lalonde, Paulin Bordeleau and Chris Oddleifson all scored 16 or more, at a time when 20 goals still meant a lot.

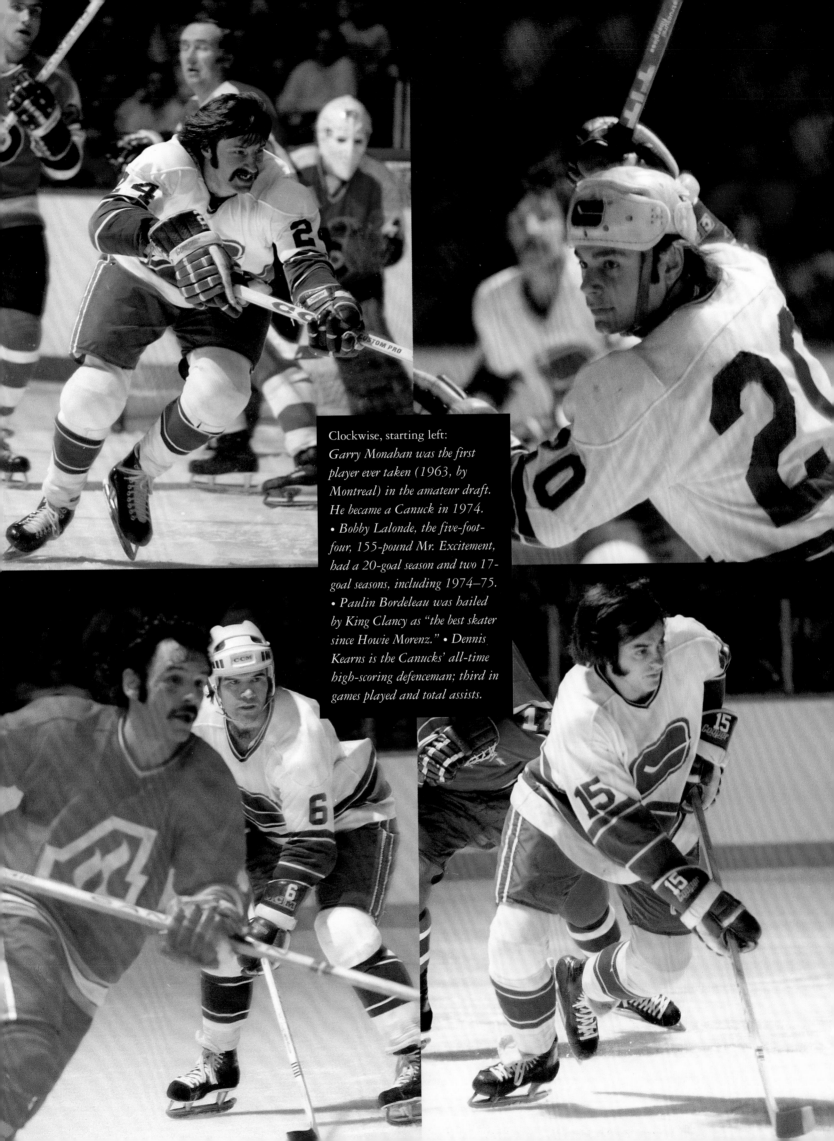

Clockwise, starting left: Garry Monahan was the first player ever taken (1963, by Montreal) in the amateur draft. He became a Canuck in 1974. • Bobby Lalonde, the five-foot-four, 155-pound Mr. Excitement, had a 20-goal season and two 17-goal seasons, including 1974–75. • Paulin Bordeleau was hailed by King Clancy as "the best skater since Howie Morenz." • Dennis Kearns is the Canucks' all-time high-scoring defenceman; third in games played and total assists.

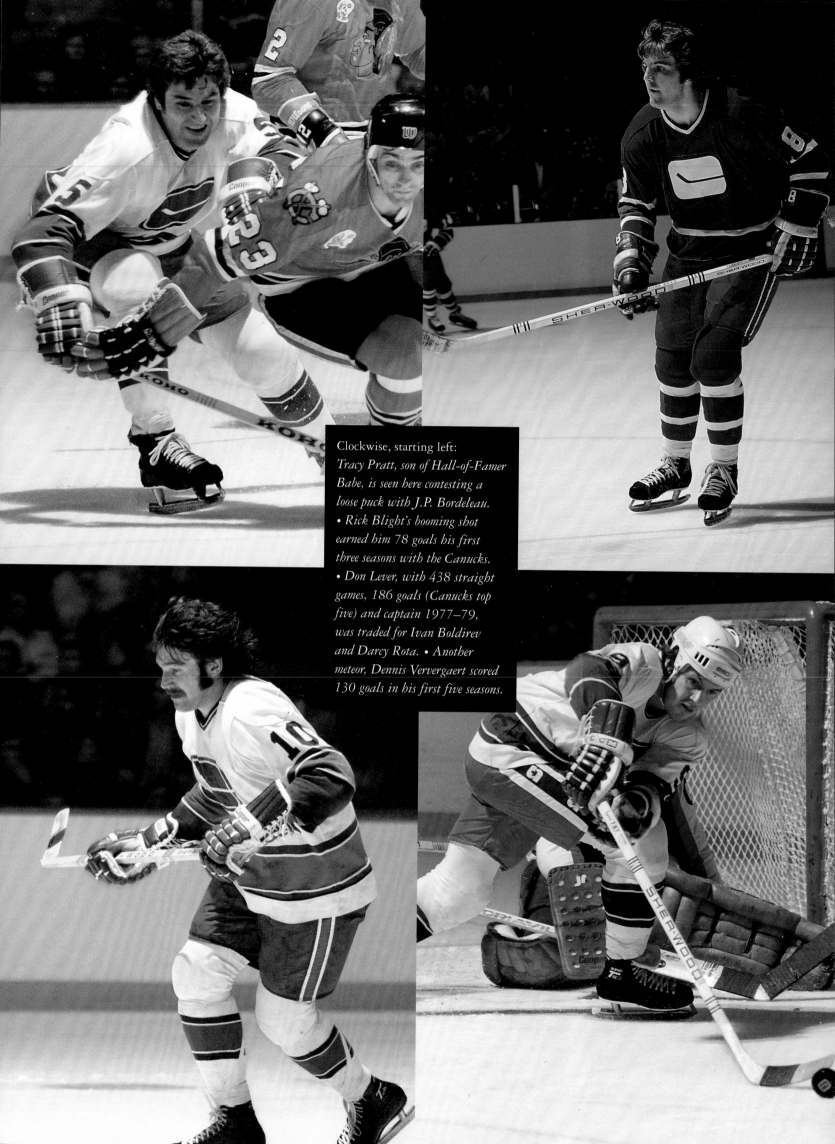

Clockwise, starting left: Tracy Pratt, son of Hall-of-Famer Babe, is seen here contesting a loose puck with J.P. Bordeleau. • Rick Blight's booming shot earned him 78 goals his first three seasons with the Canucks. • Don Lever, with 438 straight games, 186 goals (Canucks top five) and captain 1977–79, was traded for Ivan Boldirev and Darcy Rota. • Another meteor, Dennis Ververgaert scored 130 goals in his first five seasons.

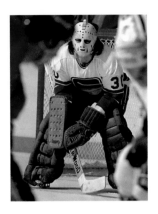

Maloney's need for a backup who could keep sharp while Gary Smith played 72 games led him to Ken "Spider" Lockett.

Cesare Maniago came to Vancouver in exchange for Gary Smith during the summer of 1976 and gave the Canucks three seasons of top-flight goaltending.

Following pages: *The defensive improvement that brought Vancouver its first NHL division championship was the blue-line partnership of Mike Robitaille and Tracy Pratt, here working over second-place St. Louis Blues' forwards, while netminder Gary Smith offers a hand.*

Still, as always in the life of a recent expansion team, the goaltender had to play the lights out. That year Gary Smith had "the best single year of any goaltender I've seen," Jim Robson, the voice of the Vancouver Canucks for 24 years, says now.

The first of Smith's six regular-season shutouts, and the one that set the tone for his lifetime season, came October 20 in New York's Madison Square Garden and gave the Canucks a 1–0 win. "The most fantastic display of goaltending I've ever seen," Maloney says. Afterward, Ranger centre Pete Stemkowski said the teams could have played until 3 am without the Rangers scoring. Asked for a comment, the fun-loving Smith replied:

"He should have seen me at three in the morning."

Gary Smith's magic continued into the playoffs. Spare goalie Ken Lockett earned the first start against the Montreal Canadiens with back-to-back shutouts April 1 and 2, but lost 6–2 in Game 1 of the playoffs.

Smith won the second game 2–1 in the Montreal Forum.

Jim Robson says the crowd at the following game in the Pacific Coliseum was the loudest he had ever heard up to that time. Smith had the Canucks in 1–1 ties, but lost both games in Vancouver, one in overtime. He posted a 3.27 average against one of the great Montreal teams, who dropped 14 games all season.

The ultimate compliment came from jillionaire Jimmy Pattison, the Blazers' owner. "I'd never met him," Maloney says. "Pattison came up to me, shook my hand, and said 'Congratulations. You did a heckuva job. You've kicked us out of town. We're going to Calgary.'"

Maloney's overachievers managed to stay one game over .500 the next season. When the team appeared to continue its gentle downward slide, Maloney promoted former captain Orland Kurtenbach, then coaching at Tulsa, to replace him behind the bench and teach such talented draftees as Don Lever (1972), Dennis Ververgaert and Bob Dailey (1973), Ron Sedlbauer and Harold Snepsts (1974), and Rick Blight (1975).

The Canucks tightened up defensively under Kurtenbach, but finished out of the playoffs, costing Maloney his job. New GM Jake Milford kept Kurtenbach, and the team opened the 1977–78 season with a 3–1–2 start, the best since that championship season. But they finished out of the playoffs for the second straight year.

Milford cleaned house.

Top: *The original Canuck jersey logo and colours, 1970–78,
worn by Captain Orland Kurtenbach in the team's inaugural
season.* Bottom: *The 1978–79 season saw a radical redesign
of the Canuck uniforms. Dave "Tiger" Williams wore this
jersey in its NHL debut.*

THE NATURAL

"An innovator with total dedication to the game," is how Jake Milford (left) introduced Harry Neale (right) to Vancouver, May 26, 1978.

Neale was that rare non-NHL player who had coached at every level – high school, college, junior and the WHA – and had figured out his own system. One of his innovations with the Canucks was to make hockey a full-time year-round occupation, letting players know his specific expectations during the summer before the season. Each player received a conditioning program.

It was a revolution. An old-line coach might have had trouble assimilating the Swedes who arrived that year or the Czechs in 1982. Neale was never afraid to hire more technically minded coaches (Tom Watt, whose first NHL job was with the Canucks, Roger Neilson or Ron Smith) and give them freedom to operate.

Neale was a natural general-manager type. His eventual downfall with the Canucks may have been the inability of the coaches he hired to keep the second-guessers at bay. Sooner or later in each case, Neale would have to step behind the bench again.

But the 1982 team that first wore Canucks colours in the Stanley Cup final, perhaps the overachievers of all time in the NHL, was his creation, and his monument.

In the spring of 1978, Harry Neale, fresh from the WHA, was introduced to the Vancouver sporting press in the most expensive suite at the Bayshore Inn as a coach who had never missed the playoffs. It was a wonderful moment for him, Neale says now – at least until he saw the new uniforms of the team he would be coaching. Designed by Beyl, Boyd and Turner, a San Francisco marketing consultancy, for a fee of $100,000, the new outfits received mixed reviews. The speeding skate crest was a classic, the colours were as aggressive as they were designed to be, but the uniform jerseys, with their big Vs on the chests and arms, were one of the first changes Pat Quinn would make at the end of the Neale era. As for Neale's playoff record, it would remain intact during his tenure with the Canucks. For six years the Canucks would finish no lower than third in the Smythe Division, but no higher than second.

Milford raised the talent level of the team with its most bountiful drafts: goaltender Glen Hanlon (1977), Bill Derlago, Curt Fraser, Stan Smyl and Gerry Minor (1978), Rick Vaive and Brent Ashton (1979), Rick Lanz, Marc Crawford, and Doug Lidster (1980), and Garth Butcher and Petri Skriko in 1981.

In 1978 Milford stole Thomas Gradin from Chicago, and in 1980 he filched netminder Richard Brodeur from the Islanders. Derlago and Vaive were packaged for Tiger Williams and Jerry Butler, and Hanlon was sacrificed for two other components (Jim Nill and Tony Currie) of the miracle that befell the Canucks in the springtime of 1982.

Clockwise, starting left:
Tiger Williams, all-time NHL penalty-minute leader, brought his winning attitude west in 1980.
• *Thomas Gradin, the Canucks' all-time best centre, 550 points in 613 games.* • *Gerry Minor, memorable as a penalty-killer, played one full year and parts of four others.* • *Ron Sedlbauer had his best years, including the first Canuck 40-goal season (1978-79), playing for Harry Neale.*

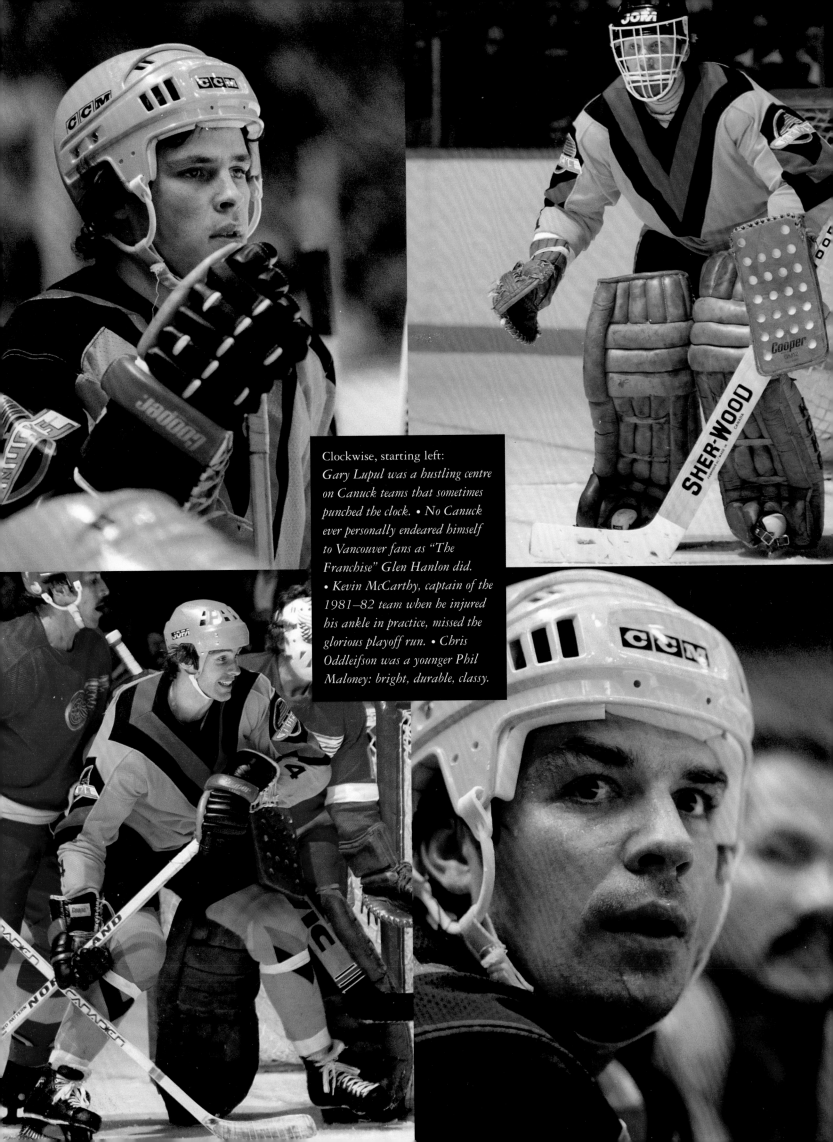

Clockwise, starting left: *Gary Lupul was a hustling centre on Canuck teams that sometimes punched the clock.* • *No Canuck ever personally endeared himself to Vancouver fans as "The Franchise" Glen Hanlon did.* • *Kevin McCarthy, captain of the 1981–82 team when he injured his ankle in practice, missed the glorious playoff run.* • *Chris Oddleifson was a younger Phil Maloney: bright, durable, classy.*

*The Clarence Campbell Bowl, named for Clarence S. Campbell,
president of the NHL from 1946 to 1977, is a hallmark piece
crafted by a British silversmith in 1879. Starting with the
1981–82 season it became emblematic of the playoff championship
of the Campbell Conference.*

The 1980s saw the NHL dynasties of the New York Islanders and the Edmonton Oilers dominate. Under the guidance of Harry Neale, the Vancouver Canucks emerged triumphant with their first Campbell Conference championship. For two magical months in 1982 they were unbeatable. That spring, Canucks fans lived the Canadian dream: the quest for the holy grail, the Stanley Cup.

The Legend

It was ironic that the single most-successful act of master motivator Harry Neale's coaching career – leaping to the aid of Tiger Williams – disqualified him from taking an active part in the first Canucks playoff to extend beyond the first round.

Neale knew that elevating Roger Neilson to head coach for the duration of the playoffs might fully exploit the team unity that had jelled in Quebec City the night of March 20.

Ron Smith is the most important link, other than the Griffiths family, between the Canucks' two Stanley Cup finalist teams. His roles with the two teams were vital – as a tactician and as the connection between the spotters upstairs and the bench.

Facing page: *The King salutes one of three victories over Chicago in May 1982, the first time the Canucks had ever played during that month.*

MARCH 20, 1982: LE COLISÉE, QUEBEC CITY, QUEBEC.

Harry Neale climbs over the glass in Quebec City, is suspended by the NHL, appoints Roger Neilson coach, and off go the Canucks to the Stanley Cup final.... So the legend goes.

Actually, there was no glass to climb at the end of the visitors' bench in Le Colisée, home of the Quebec Nordiques. This shortcoming was rectified after the incident that led to a 10-game suspension for coach Harry Neale and, many think, turned the Canucks' 1981–82 season around. There was nothing more than an aisle between that end of their bench and three rows of boardside seats.

In fact, the Canucks' season was already turned around. As Neale points out today, Vancouver was undefeated in the seven games before Neilson took over. "I tell Roger," Neale says, "if I'd been coaching, we'd have won the damn thing." The damn thing being, of course, the 1982 Stanley Cup.

But the turnaround did gain momentum when Tiger Williams ran Peter Stastny into the boards at the far end of the Vancouver bench. Tough Wilf Paiement stepped in for Stastny, pinning Williams' face to the rinkside glass.

With Tiger pinned against the glass, a fan named Pierre Fournel made his bid for fame by leaping from his fourth-row seat to take a poke at Williams.

Neale, a stout man who nevertheless ran the stairs at the Coliseum every day after practice, reacted by bounding to that end of the bench and swinging at Fournel.

"I remember thinking to myself," Neale says today, "'What the heck am I doing helping *Tiger Williams* out?'"

Neale claims his punch landed one inch short of Fournel, although no one else made that fine distinction. Defenceman Doug Halward and spare goalie Rick Heinz followed Neale, and Curt Fraser immediately began trying to make peace. Marc Crawford, who had played junior games for the Cornwall Royals in the same rink, tried to extricate Neale

The NHL was upset when the Canucks used Sen. Ray Perrault's diplomatic clout to smooth the defections of Jiri Bubla (above) and Ivan Hlinka (below). Jake Milford felt the fastest way to improve the team was to tap into a new talent pool: Czechoslovakia was the next-best option to the USSR. Czechs had always played Canadian-style hockey. Once Hlinka stopped circling into his own zone with the puck, he became a valuable addition to the Canucks' talented centre contingent: Gradin, Boldirev and Gerry Minor. Bubla soon proved to be the hardest hitter on the Canuck blue line. Hlinka averaged close to a point a game over the two seasons he suited up for the Canucks.

from the seats. Defenceman Kevin McCarthy threw a glove from the ice at a fan. Halward, a man quick to make judgements, began pummelling an individual (who did not press charges...).

Soon Roger Neilson, having shed his headphone connection with Ron Smith upstairs, was in the stands pleading for peace, "the most telltale hint of his finesse under stress with the Canucks," *The Province*'s hockey writer Tony Gallagher thought.

The game ended in a 3–3 tie, but, as Gallagher and Mike Gasher wrote in their account of that amazing season, *Towels, Triumph & Tears*, "The point they came away with was a small prize in comparison with the unity they experienced in dealing with the hostile crowd."

March 27, the night after Neale and the players involved were suspended, the Canucks, under Neilson, thrashed Calgary 7–2. Although that seventh goal was incidental to the outcome (it was scored by Tony Currie from Ivan Boldirev and Tiger Williams at 12:48 of the third period), it was the goal that would give the Canucks a 35–34 scoring edge in games between the teams – good for second place in the Smythe Division and home advantage in the playoffs.

Neale is right about when the turnaround occurred. The two games before the incident in Quebec City consisted of a loosely played March 17 6–6 tie at Washington, which marked the return of Darcy Rota's scoring touch after a seven-week absence, and a 4–2 win over Montreal the next night, with Rota scoring a hat-trick and Tiger Williams potting the winner to end the Canadiens' 27-game unbeaten streak in the Forum. Counting those games and the 3–3 tie in Quebec City, the Canucks went 17–2–3 on their way to the Campbell Conference Championship.

"We played in a way coaches dream about and players always hope they will achieve at some point in their careers," Williams wrote in *Tiger, A Hockey Story*.

"I'm not sure any team in the NHL had a better three months," Harry Neale says, "considering what kind of team we had. That, in my experience, was the greatest example of a bunch of guys who played up to and beyond their potential – and for a long time. We came to the rink absolutely positive we would win the game.

"It was more of a feeling than something you can see.

"You just know you've got it. I've had different teams in different leagues that just knew. I don't know how you do it. If I did," says *Hockey Night in Canada*'s best colour man, "I'd still have a real job."

The consummate Canuck character player, Tiger Williams:
"The problem in hockey is that you never know how long you'll
have to wait for another moment like [1982], or if it will ever

Above : *Darcy Rota still holds the club record for goals by a left winger (42 in 1982–83). His scoring touch transformed the 1981–82 Canucks into the hottest team going into that spring's playoffs.* Below: *The 1982 playoff drive may have been a triumph of lunch-bucket hockey, but slick centreman Ivan Boldirev had a 33-goal regular season and contributed a vital 8–3–11 in 17 playoff games.*

One of the cultural highlights of early 1982 was the spontaneous revival of a 1969 hit song by a Swedish group called Steam: "Na Na Hey Hey Kiss Him Goodbye." The night of April 21 during a game against the Los Angeles Kings, the crowd suddenly began singing the song, and another Vancouver playoff tradition was at hand.

Like any such outburst, this one was ripe for exploitation. Days later, enterprising former Canucks PR man Greg Douglas had organized and recorded this "Salute to the Canucks," a 45-rpm rendition of the song sung by King Richard's Army, with a ditty called "King Richard!" on the flip side. Red Robinson coordinated the advertising on the record sleeve and Peter Shelly wrote and produced the record.

One indication of the Canucks' late-season redemption was their 6–0 shutout of the Kings at Los Angeles, in the second-last game of 1981–82. The shellacking finally boosted the Canucks' goals-scored past their goals-against for the first time since the 36th game of the season – a 6–1 loss to Edmonton that began a 21-game, 2–11–8 mid-season skid. Full of themselves, with goalie Richard Brodeur feeling unbeatable, they hammered the hapless Kings 7–4 to close out the regular season.

Those two season-ending games accomplished two objectives. The Canucks were propelled into the playoffs as the hottest team in the league. And the Kings, embarrassed and driven by their hard-nosed, lifelong minor-league coach, Don Perry, upset the team that had finished 34 points clear of the Canucks, the Edmonton Oilers.

Vancouver swept the best-of-five preliminary round against the Calgary Flames. All-time Canuck games-played leader Stan Smyl scored eight seconds into the first game – a team record for fastest goal, and a score he attributes to the fact that "we buzzed them right away." Smyl hit Flames' rookie defenceman Charlie Bourgeois behind the Calgary net and, while the Flames did get the puck out of their zone, Thomas Gradin and Smyl brought it back in and immediately took advantage of Calgary's disarray. The left wing on the Gradin-Smyl line, Curt Fraser, beat up Flames heavyweight Willi Plett, "and won the series for us," in Colin Campbell's opinion. In Game 2 Brodeur and Pat Riggin duelled to a 1–1 tie through 74 minutes and 20 seconds, then Tiger Williams won it in overtime. He personally finished the Flames by checking 40-goal scorer Lanny McDonald into the ice and scoring the winner again in the third game.

In Game 3 "we beat Calgary 3–1 in one of the closest games I've ever seen," Neale remembers. "We scored into an empty net. We just got the last goal every night."

Assistant coach Ron Smith looked ahead and noted that the Canucks had paved themselves a clear, straight road to the Stanley Cup final. Smith began to see the team as divinely anointed, as early as the series against the L.A. Kings, although only after stay-at-home defenceman Colin Campbell scored twice in Game 3, April 18. The first came in the second-last minute of a first period in which Brodeur had stopped 18 shots. The second came in overtime. It doubled Campbell's six-year lifetime playoff goal-scoring total. It turned the Los Angeles series around. But Brodeur was the game's unanimous Number One Star.

TOWEL POWER IS BORN

The single most unforgettable moment in Canuck history was simply a gesture of surrender.

At the end of the first period of Game 2 of the Campbell Conference Final against the Black Hawks, April 29, 1982, the Canucks had Chicago right where they wanted them: the Hawks winning by only 1–0 after taking 19 shots on King Richard Brodeur. The King was his usual dependable self. The only worrisome aspect so far was that the Canucks were taking most of the penalties and the Hawks were taking the liberties.

Five minutes into the third period, the Canucks were losing 3–1 in a game the NHL's supervisor of officials thought couldn't have been refereed by God. A sequence of questionable calls by referee Bob Myers, including a Curt Fraser goal called back, put a close game out of reach for the Canucks.

"I was sitting near [coach Roger] Neilson," Tiger Williams wrote later, "and I pointed to the stick rack and said, 'Let's throw every frigging stick on the ice,' and he said 'No, I already did that one time. Let's surrender.' Then he raised the white towel.

"Gerry Minor... and I grabbed some towels and joined in, and the whole situation just ignited. The photographs went all over North America, and a lot of people decided that Neilson must be pretty near a damned genius. I said to some of the guys, 'Didn't I tell you he was a pretty smart guy?'"

Myers, true to form, might have been the last in Chicago Stadium to notice. Neilson hoisted his towel on Jim Nill's stick just as the teams came to centre ice for a faceoff.

From what might otherwise have been a disastrous shift of momentum in the series, Neilson gained the psychological edge. The Hawks thought his gesture of surrender had won them the series. The Canucks proved otherwise.

It was during the last game of the Kings series that the first of Pacific Coliseum playoff traditions originated. *Na Na Na Na, Hey Hey, Goodbye* bubbled up out of the sheer exuberance that being released from a dozen years of frustration visited upon 16,000 souls all at once. Like other near-forgotten rock anthems that have found new life in hockey arenas, "Na Na Hey Hey Kiss Him Goodbye" soon became a victory song.

Brodeur won Game 1 of the Campbell Conference Championship against Chicago by prolonging an early 1–1 tie for 78 minutes and 47 seconds; stopping 46 shots, including a flurry of Hawk chances at the stroke of midnight; and sending the Canucks into a second overtime that newcomer Jim Nill finished by roofing a Snepsts point-shot rebound. It was, up to then, the longest game and biggest win in Canuck history.

Two days later came the franchise's best-remembered loss and Roger Neilson's finest hour. Late in a third period in which referee Bob Myers fumbled what should have been a tight 3–2 game into a 4–1 foregone conclusion after disallowing a Canuck goal and awarding the Hawks their ninth man-advantage, Neilson saved his team's dignity by hoisting a towel on Nill's stick in a gesture of surrender.

By the end of Game 3, when the Hawks felt themselves victimized by the officials, their response – coach Bob Pulford harangued Andy vanHellemond and Denis Savard spat at him – made it clear the Canucks had won the war of nerves and the series.

The most indelible moving image from that playoff run, though, is King Richard Brodeur, the shy, reclusive doughboy from Longueuil, Quebec, who owned Vancouver from the first week of April to mid-May that spring when anything seemed possible. Brodeur stepped out of the solitude of his net and attacked the shooters during the most glorious stretch of his NHL career. Time after time, pads together, head up, he would make the critical save out near the rim of the faceoff circle and turn the rebound harmlessly to the side, brimming with confidence that his patchwork defence was covering everyone but the puck carrier. And it did. If he had to freeze the puck, what seemed to be his own television camera would follow him on his tension-releasing skate to the corner and back while the teams lined up for the resulting faceoff. Stan Smyl, captain (with Kevin McCarthy injured for the playoffs), once skated out to congratulate his goalie after an especially momentous save and was surprised to see King Richard grinning inside his mask. He was having the time of his life.

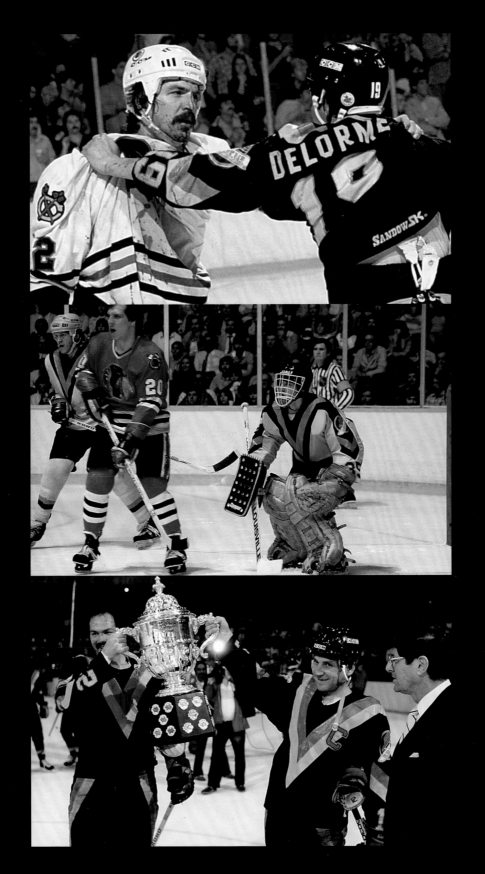

Top: *Grant Mulvey makes peace with "Chief" Ron Delorme in the
battle of the heavyweights.* Centre: *King Richard is partially screened
by Chicago's Al Secord, with Lars Lindgren keeping an eye on things.*
Bottom: *Harold Snepsts and Stan Smyl, forever in our hearts, hoist
the Canucks' first-ever Campbell Conference Trophy, 1981–82.*

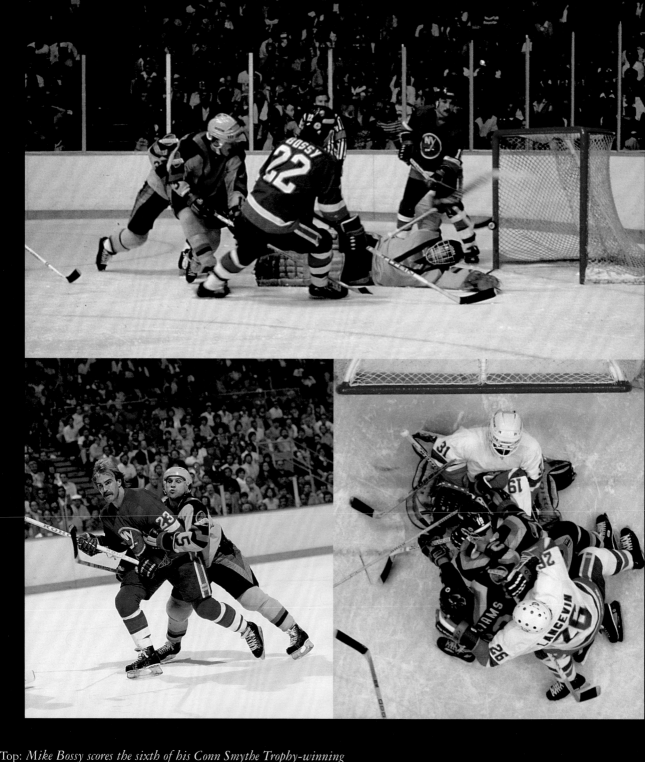

Top: *Mike Bossy scores the sixth of his Conn Smythe Trophy-winning seven goals to beat the Vancouver Canucks 3–1 and win the 1982 Stanley Cup.* Bottom left: *Colin Campbell became a scoring threat during the 1982 playoff run, but took care of his other duties as well. Here he giftwraps Bob Nystrom.* Bottom right: *In-your-face hockey: Tiger Williams and Ron Delorme crowd Billy Smith's net and are held there by Islander defenceman Dave Langevin.*

"*Thanks for making all of us winners*," *says the engraving on a trophy presented to the Canucks by Vancouver city council in May 1982. Half a million people showed up to watch the team ride down Burrard Street to Sunset Beach, a fact that Tim Hunter, then with Calgary, noted with wonder.*

The first time the Stanley Cup was paraded around the Pacific Coliseum, it was not in the hands of a Vancouver Canuck.

The Canucks might have won the first two games of the Stanley Cup final played on Long Island. Thomas Gradin scored a minute and a half into the first game, which was lost with two seconds left in the first overtime period when Harold Snepsts, of all people, coughed up the puck.

Tiger Williams watched the sad tableau from the boards. Snepsts, behind his own net, first tried to move the puck to him, but Williams shouted No! He was covered. Snepsts saw Gerry Minor signal for a pass up the middle, but resisted that temptation. He tried to loft the puck out of the zone. He just didn't get it high enough.

Mike Bossy was waiting in the slot. The greatest sniper of his time, he knocked the puck down and clanged it off the shocked Brodeur's right goalpost.

Long after everyone else had dressed, Snepsts, the Canucks' all-time fan favourite, was sitting alone in his sweat-soaked gear in a small trainer's room, his head in his hands. "That could have happened to anyone," Tiger Williams would write.

After some time, "I went to Harold," Neale recalls, "and I said 'The bus is leaving. Get your equipment off and we love the way you're playing.'

"Then I went to [equipment manager] Ken Fleger and told him to get Harold out of there, even if it had to be with his skates on."

Fleger took Snepsts to Oyster Bay, Long Island, where the big defence-man spent the predawn hours walking the beach.

In Game 2 the Canucks went into the third period with a one-goal lead after playing their best period of the series.

Power play opportunities caused by an overly aggressive Curt Fraser and a reputation penalty on Tiger Williams called by referee Ron Wicks gave the Islanders a one-goal lead, and Bob Nystrom scored the insurance goal with less than six minutes left to ice the victory. "Then," says Neale, "we found out how good the Islanders were when they came to our rink. Bossy, Trottier, Potvin, Smith....

"It's a magnificent obsession, to win the Stanley Cup. If you don't have more guys than the opposition who think their lives are on the line, you're in danger of losing."

And they did. In four straight. If there is any consolation to that brave bunch of Vancouver Canucks who first made us all winners, it is this: One year later, the Islanders swept the Edmonton Oilers too.

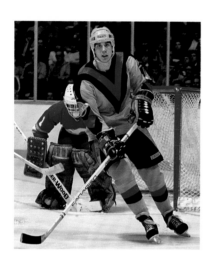

It was never seen as a long-term solution, and all anyone can say now is that it seemed like a good idea at the time. Barry Pederson, like Chris Oddleifson before him, played well but could not be the franchise player the Canucks hoped for in 1986. Remember the teenaged Cam Neely? Every goal he scored for Boston in Vancouver was a fan's moment of despair. It was not just the loss of the kid from Maple Ridge: The draft choice Boston exacted for Pederson brought them Glen Wesley. If any single move indicated the need for the change that brought Pat Quinn to Vancouver, it was the Cam Neely deal.

Jake Milford never got credit for building the team that went to the 1982 Stanley Cup final. Every player on the team except Harold Snepsts was acquired by Milford. He scoured the hockey-playing world to find them.

"There's always a tendency when that happens" – when a team suddenly starts to win – "to forget how those guys got there," said St. Louis Blues then-president Emile "The Cat" Francis later that year, tipping his hat to Milford, his 15-year colleague in the Rangers organization.

It came naturally to Milford to look far and wide for players. He turned pro in 1935 with the London Monarchs, whose road trips included Paris, Prague and Berlin. After winning the American League title in 1941 with Cleveland, he joined the RCAF and became a bombardier in Halifax bombers over Germany. Finding talent in Sweden and Czechoslovakia was nothing new for him.

By previous arrangement, Harry Neale became GM in the fall of 1982. When Neale was forced back downstairs to replace Roger Neilson on January 19, 1984, and then Bill Laforge on November 21, 1984, he was succeeded as GM by Jack Gordon, who had been Milford's assistant since 1980. It was Gordon who traded Cam Neely to Boston for Barry Pederson in 1986.

It was clear the organization was due for another overhaul. Arthur Griffiths, who had been learning on the job with Milford as tutor, went looking for someone to take control.

His first choice was Dave King, coach of the Canadian National Team. His second choice was Pat Quinn, the stay-at-home defenceman of the original NHL Canuck team who, since that time, had been captain of the Atlanta Flames and Coach of the Year with the Flyers, had become a lawyer, and had revived the Los Angeles Kings in 1984.

Griffiths discovered when he looked for Quinn's contract in the registry at league headquarters that the contract was not listed there.

Unregistered management-personnel contracts are invitations for offers. When they hired him, the Kings had agreed not to register Quinn's. That meant he might be available.

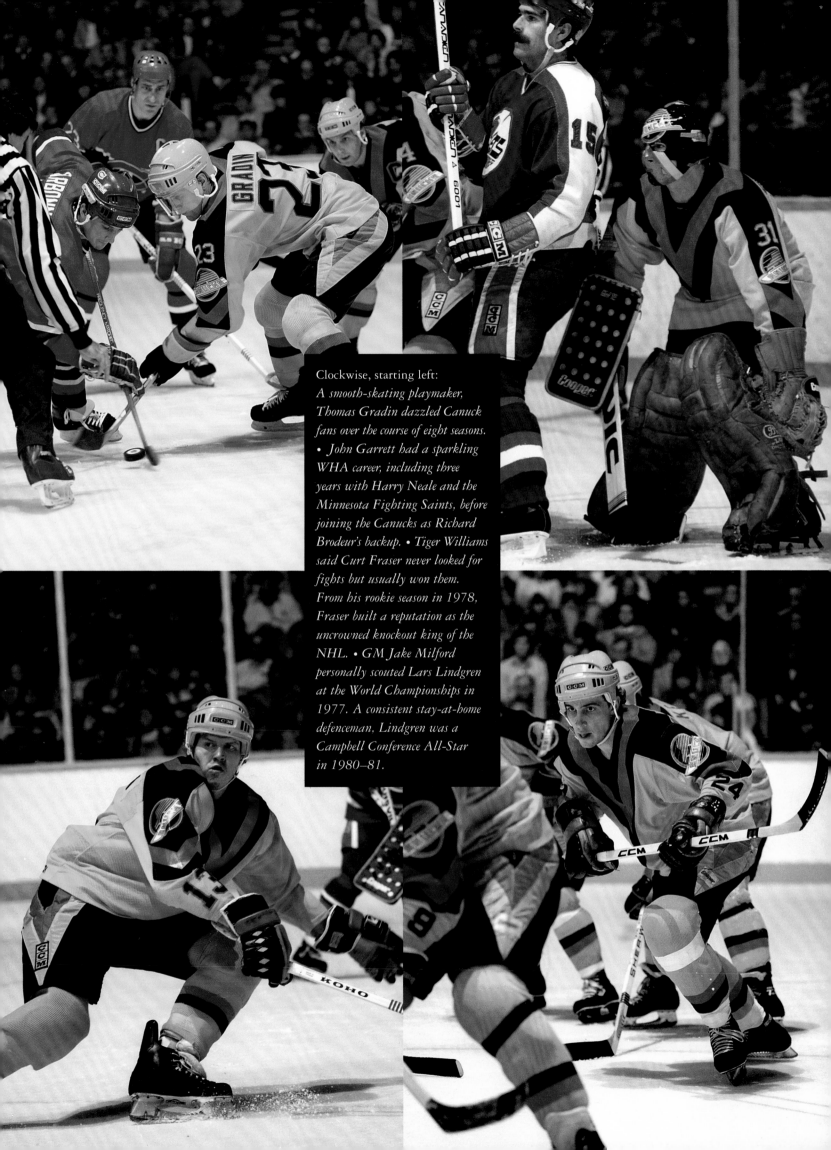

Clockwise, starting left:
A smooth-skating playmaker, Thomas Gradin dazzled Canuck fans over the course of eight seasons. • John Garrett had a sparkling WHA career, including three years with Harry Neale and the Minnesota Fighting Saints, before joining the Canucks as Richard Brodeur's backup. • Tiger Williams said Curt Fraser never looked for fights but usually won them. From his rookie season in 1978, Fraser built a reputation as the uncrowned knockout king of the NHL. • GM Jake Milford personally scouted Lars Lindgren at the World Championships in 1977. A consistent stay-at-home defenceman, Lindgren was a Campbell Conference All-Star in 1980–81.

*The Jack Adams Award commemorates the builder of the great
Detroit Red Wing teams of the late 1940s and 1950s, and
is awarded to the coach judged by the NHL Broadcasters'
Association "to have contributed the most to his team's success."*

Sixteen years after the Vancouver Canucks' inaugural season, Arthur Griffiths set out on a mission: to find the right man to build the franchise into a winner. He knew he needed an experienced and respected hockey man who could lead not only the team but the whole organization into the future. That future, Griffiths believed, would be much brighter with the right man at the helm.

Stealing Pat Quinn

With lessons as fresh as the fifth-place division finish in 1987–88 and the 42 goals Cam Neely scored for Boston that year, the Canucks' draft decision was simplified: Trevor Linden, a big winger with a lot of potential. Any complaints?

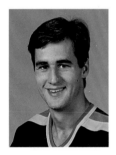 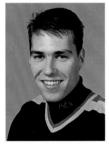

Joining the Canucks in the 1989 trade for Patrik Sundstrom, Greg Adams (left) and Kirk McLean (right) became key components of Pat Quinn's master plan.

Facing page: *Pat Quinn saw great team-builders up close and learned there is no one way to do it. Bud Poile (Flyers and Canucks); Cliff Fletcher (Atlanta, Calgary, Toronto); and Keith Allen (Philadelphia) taught him to do* everything *right – scout whatever moves, add character, watch the waiver wire, seek tomorrow's star.*

DECEMBER 24, 1986: LOS ANGELES, CALIFORNIA.

That night, Christmas Eve, Los Angeles Kings coach Pat Quinn signed a contract to become the Canucks' general manager after the season. Kings owner Jerry Buss cried foul, the Canucks were fined $310,000 by NHL president John Ziegler and Quinn was suspended from coaching in the NHL until 1990.

In other words, Quinn was signing to take a different job with a different organization when his contractual obligation with the Kings ceased. It is important to remember that Pat Quinn is a lawyer. The arrangement was carefully researched, and was upheld in B.C. Supreme Court in late 1987. The penalties against Quinn and the Canucks were overturned.

At the time, Quinn was halfway through the last year of his contract. The Kings had hired the big Irishman in 1984 on the understanding that he would succeed Kings GM Rogie Vachon. But they failed to exercise an option in Quinn's contract to offer him the GM's job after two years or allow him to entertain offers. Quinn, meanwhile, improved the Kings' standing by 23 points in his first year there.

"In fact, they didn't talk to me at all," he remembers. His wife, Sandra, hated Los Angeles. They decided to move back to Philadelphia after the season, where he would practise law.

Arthur Griffiths contacted Quinn's advisor, Dick Babush, to see whether Quinn would be interested in rejoining the Canucks as general manager when his contract expired.

"I said, 'Yeah, pursue it, see what they're talking about.'"

Griffiths made an offer to Babush on December 10, then he and Quinn met in San Diego. Quinn wanted clarification of his powers with the Canucks. Arthur was happy to tell him he would be the team's superboss, a position the Griffiths had been trying to fill for years.

B.C. BOYS

How utterly novel. Recruiting local kids for the city's NHL team – what will Pat Quinn think of next?

There have been British Columbians on most Canuck teams. But the majority by far were from the prairies, Quebec, or the big cities of Ontario.

B.C. became a hockey talent greenhouse in the early '70s. Danny Gare, Cam Neely, Andy Moog and Brett Hull (although born in Belleville, he learned his hockey in North Vancouver) are all from B.C. Darcy Rota is from Prince George. Stan Smyl, from Alberta, is a product of the New Westminster Bruins' Memorial Cup teams.

During the Canucks' rebuilding years, Pat Quinn noticed that some players jumped at the chance to join – the ones who had lived through the 1982 playoff run, like Geoff Courtnall and Cliff Ronning.

By 1991 five Canuck regulars had grown up watching the Canucks: Greg Adams of Nelson, Courtnall of Victoria, Doug Lidster of Kamloops, Ronning of Burnaby, and Ryan Walter of Burnaby, who replaced the crowd-pleasing Steve Bozek *(below)* of Castlegar on the Canuck roster that year. Nathan LaFayette has replaced Lidster on the current roster.

More are on the way. Centre Dan Kesa is from Vancouver. The Canucks' 1994 draft had a distinctly B.C. flavour, with Cloverdale's Robb Gordon and Salmon Arm's Dave Scathard taken in the second and third rounds.

"It's funny, the timing of it," Quinn says now. In response to his requests for status clarification with the Kings, they had offered him a contract extension – but as coach, not GM. The Canucks played at Los Angeles December 21, and Quinn and the Griffiths brothers, Frank Jr. and Arthur, met to finalize the details of the contract. That night the Canucks won 6–2 on the ice, and off the ice began building themselves a front office for the 1990s.

Quinn signed as VP and GM of the Canucks, accepting a $100,000 signing bonus to seal the deal. "The next day I reported – and here was the mistake – I reported this to Rogie. I planned to stay. I felt I was obligated to the owners and players to fulfill my contract [with L.A.].

"The Canucks contract was simply a futures contract. [Until I signed it] I had no contract after this [the Kings contract]. I wasn't going to be coaching [with Vancouver]. I said, 'I'll be the best coach that I can be for you guys.'

"That's when [Kings owner Jerry] Buss called and said, 'Can you change your mind? I want to keep you here.' I said, 'I fully warned your assistant [Vachon], and you had every opportunity to fulfill your obligation to me, but I never heard from you. I have no contract with you after the end of this season. I do have a contract with Vancouver.'

"That was when [then-NHL president John] Ziegler found it in his wisdom that I couldn't do my job as coach of one club when I was signed to take another position with another club for the following season."

Ziegler's implication, of course, was that Quinn would somehow be a lesser coach with the Kings because of his future commitment to manage the Canucks. It shortchanged the competitiveness of the Griffiths family, who had embarked upon their second major top-to-bottom overhaul of the club. And it was an insult to Quinn, a coach with a .602 lifetime winning percentage after making the Kings winners in 1984. That implication was the crux of the Vancouver club's suit against the NHL in B.C. Supreme Court the following October.

The late Frank Griffiths, under cross-examination, was asked to comment on what might have transpired if the contract had remained secret. Queried the NHL's lawyer, "[If] Vancouver had won the fourth playoff spot and Los Angeles did not make the playoffs, and this deal was later disclosed, that would affect the public's perception of the level of competition in the league, wouldn't it?"

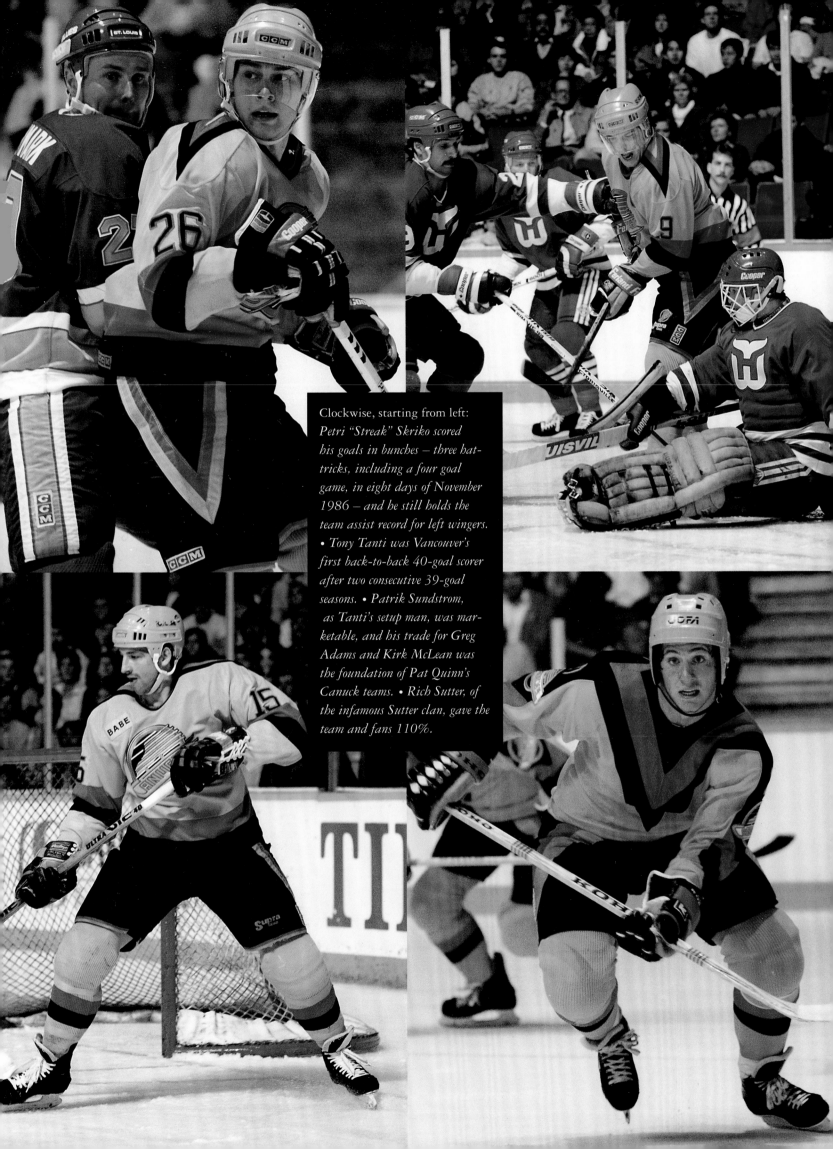

Clockwise, starting from left: Petri "Streak" Skriko scored his goals in bunches — three hat-tricks, including a four goal game, in eight days of November 1986 — and he still holds the team assist record for left wingers. • Tony Tanti was Vancouver's first back-to-back 40-goal scorer after two consecutive 39-goal seasons. • Patrik Sundstrom, as Tanti's setup man, was marketable, and his trade for Greg Adams and Kirk McLean was the foundation of Pat Quinn's Canuck teams. • Rich Sutter, of the infamous Sutter clan, gave the team and fans 110%.

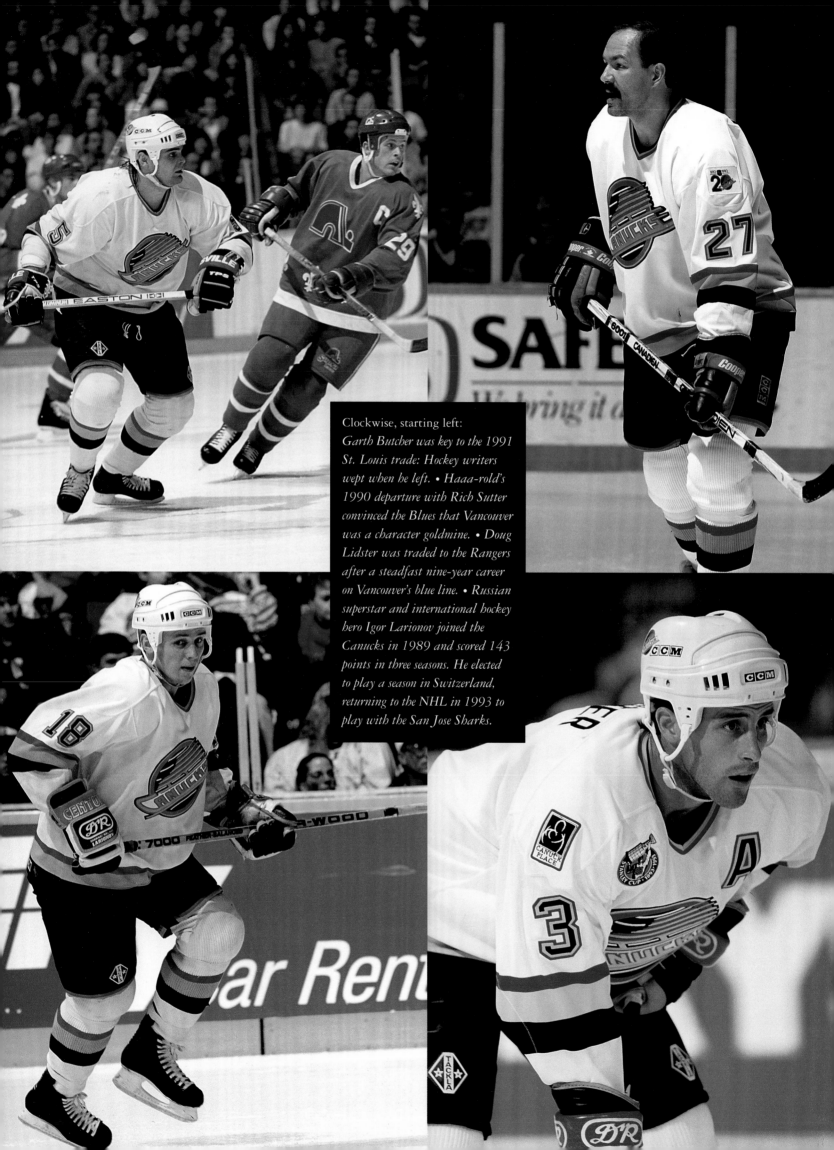

Clockwise, starting left:
Garth Butcher was key to the 1991 St. Louis trade: Hockey writers wept when he left. • Haaa-rold's 1990 departure with Rich Sutter convinced the Blues that Vancouver was a character goldmine. • Doug Lidster was traded to the Rangers after a steadfast nine-year career on Vancouver's blue line. • Russian superstar and international hockey hero Igor Larionov joined the Canucks in 1989 and scored 143 points in three seasons. He elected to play a season in Switzerland, returning to the NHL in 1993 to play with the San Jose Sharks.

In reuniting two-thirds of the Soviet Union's fabled K-L-M Line, the Canucks hoped both Igor Larionov (left) and left winger Vladimir Krutov (right) could adjust to western life. "I left for one reason," Larionov said in his 1990 autobiography, published the year he joined the Canucks, "freedom to choose my own path." But Krutov's inability to function apart from the year-round Central Red Army system limited him to a single year in the NHL. Larionov's lasting contribution to the Canucks was taking Pavel Bure under his wing when the Russian Rocket arrived in 1991.

Paul Reinhart extended his career by coming to Vancouver and provided the Canucks with the powerplay quarterback the team had lacked for so long, with 90 assists in two years.

"If he is as knowledgeable a fan as you suggest," Griffiths replied, "he could judge by the level of play and the effect on Quinn's [bonus provisions in his Kings] contract if he did not make the playoffs. He would see that Quinn would want to leave behind a winning record and not be seen as a lame duck."

Exactly. It was the idea that the team ownership would lower the level of competition in the NHL by hiring Pat Quinn that made it necessary to take the case to court. And win.

To many fans, Pat Quinn's first move was the trade for Greg Adams and Kirk McLean. But there were things to be done before he could start working the phones to rebuild the team.

The first was to hire Brian Burke. They met in 1978, Quinn's first year as a coach and Burke's first as a professional hockey player – a hockey player who had been accepted into Harvard Law School. They stayed in touch. Burke loaned Quinn his law textbooks. Burke represented players on Quinn's Kings teams. Burke's current status as the NHL's VP for Hockey Operations is evidence of the Canuck boss's eye for talent.

Next Quinn hired Bob McCammon, the coach he replaced with Philadelphia in 1978, and the coach who replaced him with the same team in 1981–82. After all that, they still got along.

Now he could get down to work. "The Canucks had a cadre of pretty good players," he says. "Tony Tanti, who I thought could be a consistent 40-goal scorer, Stan Smyl, Patrik Sundstrom, Barry Pederson, Petri Skriko. After them, the skill level dropped off dramatically. We were big and slow on defence. Our skilled players couldn't get the puck.

"My goal wasn't to get one quality guy for one quality guy. It was to get two or three lesser prospects for one quality guy."

The most marketable player was Sundstrom. In fact, trading the Swedish centre was Quinn's fourth player transaction, not his first. As for the players he got for Sundstrom, McLean and Adams, "they've been everything we hoped they would be." Maybe more.

One benefit of the Canucks' slow decline during Harry Neale's last couple of years was the first opportunity since the franchise's founding to draft as high as second overall in 1988. (The Canucks had the number three pick from 1971 to 1973.) There was a clear choice to be made in that talent-rich draft. The Canucks could have taken an instant impact player, of which several were available, or a longer-term project with leadership potential. The decision was to be patient.

DRAFTING PAVEL

June 17, 1989, National Hockey League amateur draft, sixth round. The Canucks had already gambled on two high-school prospects when chief scout Mike Penny, one of about a dozen men at the Vancouver table, thought they should take an even bigger one.

"Take Bure," he said.

It was a bold move. At that time, Europeans drafted after the third round had to have played 11 games at their country's elite level. Had Pavel played that many games for Central Red Army? Penny thought so. He was certainly the best player still available.

During the 1988–89 season he had been rookie of the year in the Soviet Elite League and top forward at the World Junior Championships in Anchorage. He had led the Soviets to the gold medal and scored 8–6–14 on a line with Sergei Fedorov and Alexander Mogilny.

Any team could have taken him in the first three rounds. Twenty-five teams passed on Pavel Bure through five rounds. "We didn't know if we would ever get him," Penny says now. "What was more difficult to get than a release from the Red Army [in those days]?"

"Take him." Penny repeated. Nobody at the table argued. "He's the best player available."

"When you watch Bure play," Penny says now, "it's gratifying."

Gratifying? Back-to-back 60-goal seasons: that's gratification.

Facing page: This 1992–93 bench shows how much the Canucks lineup changed in two seasons. Of the 13 players pictured, five – Robert Kron, Garry Valk, Petr Nedved, Jim Sandlak and Dixon Ward – were gone by the 1994 playoffs. Adrien Plavsic, while still with the team, did not play. Assistant coach Ron Wilson (headphones) is head coach for the Anaheim Mighty Ducks.

Leaving such players as Curtis Leschyshyn, Jeremy Roenick, Teemu Selanne and Rod Brind'Amour in the pool, Quinn took Trevor Linden, a big winger from Medicine Hat. Some say he was the best draft choice since Garth Butcher.

The next year, 1989, Quinn and his scouting team would take the impact player they hadn't been ready for the year before – Pavel Bure.

Pat Quinn emphasized throughout the Canucks rebuilding process that it would require patience. It would do no good, for example, to draft a future superstar and have him step into the wrong environment. Even as recently as 1991, Quinn was saying it would be years before his program could be judged.

When the Canucks drew Calgary as opponents in the first round of the 1994 playoffs, comparisons were made between the 1989 Canucks team that took Calgary to overtime in the seventh game and the current one. Both Vancouver teams – 1989 and 1994 – were considered underdogs.

But those two Canucks teams were vastly different in makeup and attitude. The core of the 1989 team included Paul Reinhart, Petri Skriko and Tony Tanti, three of the team's four top scorers. Robert Nordmark played 80 games, Rich Sutter 75, Jim Sandlak 72, Brian Bradley and Steve Bozek 71, Jim Benning 65, Barry Pederson 62 and David Bruce 53. Trevor Linden, in his rookie season, scored 30 times to tie for the team lead in goals and become the team's second-highest point-scorer. An overtime breakaway by Stan Smyl, playing his second-last season, became the moment for Mike Vernon's Stanley Cup save.

On the whole, these players don't match up with their replacements. Bure, of course, is the main upgrade. In Pavel Bure the Canucks franchise has its first marquee player, the first to be paid in the same range as the league's elite. All the 1994 Canucks' key players, except Linden, McLean and Adams, have been added since 1989: Sergio Momesso, Geoff Courtnall, Robert Dirk (now with Anaheim) and Cliff Ronning, who came from St. Louis on March 5, 1991. Jyrki Lumme was a late-season 1990 theft from Montreal's then-surplus of defencemen. Quinn's gambling draft pick of 1990, Petr Nedved, indirectly brought Jeff Brown, Bret Hedican and Nathan LaFayette on March 22, 1994. In a complex deal, Robert Kron and Jim Sandlak were exchanged for Murray Craven of Hartford.

WHO'S GOT THE BLUES?
It's almost a formula. Want the Canucks to go to the Stanley Cup final? Dial (314) 555-RON!, and ask for Ron Caron.

These trades just keep getting better and better. To begin with, Caron is a great judge of hockey talent. His teams are stacked but they underachieve. He is forever seeking the character factor.

Looking back on it, the original St. Louis trade (March 9, 1982) may have been one-sided in the Blues' favour. Whatever psychological effect it had on the Canucks in their 1982 playoff drive, the players they received for Glen Hanlon had little permanent value. Rick Heinz, the goalie loaned as backup to Richard Brodeur, was returned to St. Louis after the season. Both Jim Nill and Tony Currie were gone by early 1984. Nill did bring Peter McNab in trade.

The March 5, 1991 trade was a near-desperation move after Pat Quinn thought he saw the Canucks quit in an 8–0 blowout at the hands of the Blackhawks March 3, 1991, on the heels of 9–1 (Kings) and 7–1 (Canadiens) losses. Of Sergio Momesso, Cliff Ronning, Robert Dirk and Geoff Courtnall, only Dirk is gone. (Later the same day, Quinn acquired Dana Murzyn, his best defenceman in 1993–94.) Alas, the Canucks exited early from the playoffs that year.

The contributions of Jeff Brown, Bret Hedican and Nathan LaFayette to the 1994 drive to the Stanley Cup final are well known.

None of these trades were one-sided deals. In 1982 the Blues got Glen Hanlon, once "The Franchise" in Vancouver. In 1991 the bait was Garth Butcher, one of the best first-round draft picks the Canucks ever made. In March 1994 it was Petr Nedved (*above*) or Craig Janney. Either way, it was a good trade.

The most dramatic change over those years is the assembly of an airtight defence – Dave Babych, Gerald Diduck, Brian Glynn – that was once referred to as "Quinn's bargain-basement defence." In Game 5 of the 1994 Calgary series, Trevor Linden became the centre the Canucks had been looking for all that time.

In contrast, Calgary has stood still since 1989. That season's Flames were a team that could afford not to dress two of these three players: Jim Peplinski (their captain), Tim Hunter (assistant captain) and sure Hall-of-Famer Lanny McDonald. That team had also recently added Doug Gilmour.

It was Calgary assistant coach Tom Watt's unenviable job to tell two of the Flames leaders they would not play in any given playoff game that spring. Those two would dress and warm up as if they were playing, stand up and give a cheer as the team left the dressing room, then strip to their underwear and watch the first period from the dressing room while they worked out on stationary bikes. "Two out of three captains not dressing but working out," Harry Neale points out. "You wonder why they won the Stanley Cup?"

The 1989 Canucks did not have that kind of surplus talent. The 1994 team, on the other hand, had some fairly impressive talent waiting to step in, as Brian Glynn did when Dana Murzyn was injured. Like the 1989 series against Calgary, the epic 1994 series went to a seventh-game overtime. As was the case in the 1989 Vancouver–Calgary classic, the better team barely won.

Previous pages: *What goes around, comes around: Trevor Linden gives future teammate Murray Craven, then with Hartford, a stiff shove as Cliff Ronning zeroes in on the puck.*

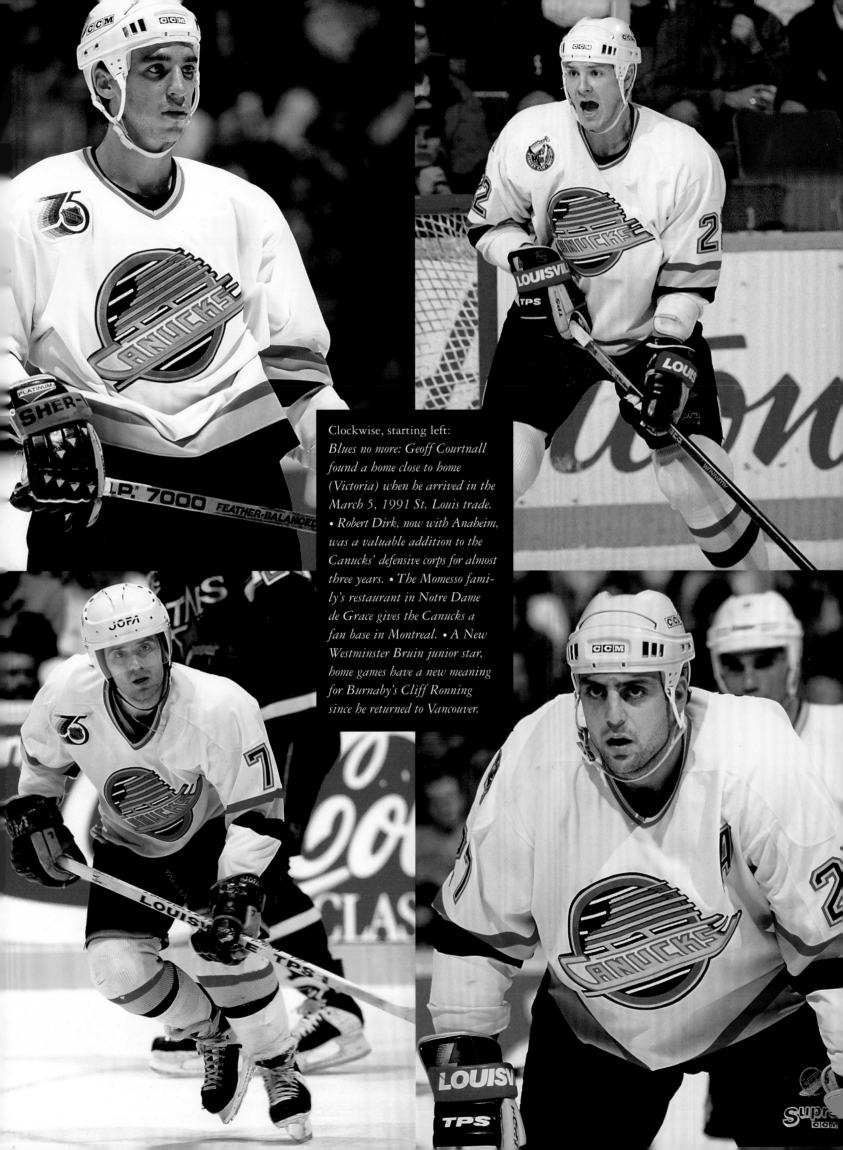

Clockwise, starting left:

Blues no more: Geoff Courtnall found a home close to home (Victoria) when he arrived in the March 5, 1991 St. Louis trade. • *Robert Dirk, now with Anaheim, was a valuable addition to the Canucks' defensive corps for almost three years.* • *The Momesso family's restaurant in Notre Dame de Grace gives the Canucks a fan base in Montreal.* • *A New Westminster Bruin junior star, home games have a new meaning for Burnaby's Cliff Ronning since he returned to Vancouver.*

Top: *Arthur Griffiths joins Pat Quinn with his second Jack Adams Award, and Pavel Bure, with the Canucks' first-ever Calder Memorial Trophy for rookie of the year.* Bottom left: *The successes of 1990–91 and 1991–92 paid off, not only in silverware, but in All-Star appearances for Kirk McLean and Trevor Linden.* Bottom right: *Washington's captain and owner of a Stanley Cup ring with Montreal, Burnaby's Ryan Walter returned home for two consecutive first-place finishes.*

Clockwise, starting left: *Kay Whitmore's won-lost record over two years is 36–22–4.* • *Adrien Plavsic was second among Canuck defencemen in scoring in 1992–93 with 6–21–27 in 57 games.* • *Jiri Slegr, a regular on the Czech national team at 18, became the first son of a former Canuck – Jiri Bubla – to wear a Vancouver uniform.* • *Gino Odjick had a career year in 1993–94, 16–13–29 with five game-winners and the second-best plus minus on the team, +13.* Facing page: *The Russian Rocket in full flight: 154 goals in 224 games over three seasons. Only Wayne Gretzky and Mike Bossy exceeded these totals in their first three seasons. Need we say more?*

As the National Hockey League has grown since 1967, the quest for the Stanley Cup has become less a test of skill than of self-sacrifice — two full months or longer during which injuries never heal and the pace of play only quickens. In the NHL, having your name on the Cup is the only thing that counts.

Along the road to the Stanley Cup, the Calgary Flames, Dallas Stars and Toronto Maple Leafs fell to a Canuck team that had come together and excelled beyond all expectations in the playoffs. The Canucks' journey covered 37 days, 17 playoff games, six overtime games, 12 wins and five losses, culminating in a face-to-face encounter with the regular season's best — the New York Rangers. And the Stanley Cup finals began...

The Stanley Cup Final

The Canucks faced the media inquisition in New York on a daily basis. The media's quest for a story often targeted Bure, Linden and McLean as victims of the obvious: "Your thoughts on the Stanley Cup...?"

Facing page: *Greg Adams, always the timely scorer, wins the first game of the Stanley Cup final in Madison Square Garden with 34 seconds left in the first overtime.*

MAY 28, 1994. NEW YORK CITY.

DESTINATION: MADISON SQUARE GARDEN.

The Vancouver Canucks arrived in Manhattan for the first two games of the Stanley Cup final and found themselves on another planet. The New York papers, bursting with the exploits of the basketball Knicks and the Yankees, had pretty much awarded the Cup to the Rangers. This was understandable, but premature.

If anything, it gave the Canucks an edge. By now they had proven to themselves they could win it. They believed they were tougher and more accustomed to transcontinental travel. The longer they could make the series last, they believed, the more likely they were to win it.

It was handy to have employed the other team's most recent coach going into a Stanley Cup final. Ron Smith, who fit into the recent New York coaching merry-go-round between Roger Neilson and Mike Keenan, felt that "looking at them, knowing them fairly well, I believed we had a good chance of beating them in six."

Throughout the playoffs, Kirk McLean was absorbing instruction from sportswriters about how to play his position. No matter that goaltenders are mysteries to even the best coaches. The sportswriters knew better. They reminded him that all Stanley Cup champions have great goaltenders. He was advised to be more aggressive with his stick, like the Islanders' Billy Smith 10 years before, to fight off the Gary Robertses of this world. And he was counselled that, for the Canucks to have any chance at all, he would have to steal a game or two.

Game 1: May 31, 1994. Madison Square Garden, New York.

Canucks 3–2 in OT. McLean takes the reporters' advice. Game 1 is a good time to do so. McLean likes playing in New York. Madison Square Garden's lighting is less intense than the Pacific Coliseum's. The television lights high above the Coliseum's press box cast shadows. McLean feels that Madison Square Garden has a smaller ice surface, which enables him to play deeper in his net. The end boards are

Dave Babych congratulates Kirk McLean on his spectacular Game 1, 52-save performance.

Bret Hedican, Martin Gelinas, Sergio Momesso and Cliff Ronning celebrate after Gelinas poked Ronning's rebound past Ranger goalie Mike Richter to tie Game 1 in the last minute of regulation.

more rounded than in Vancouver, making shoot-arounds easier to control behind the net.

The on-ice choreography between a goaltender and his team is a delicate thing, splendid to behold when it works, embarrassing when it doesn't. The team whose goalie seems unbeatable moves the puck faster and plays to win. Penalties? No problem. So McLean knew full well, when he decided to steal the first game in New York, that when the rest of the Canucks got the message, anything would be possible.

And it was. McLean's masterpiece changed the tenor of the New York sporting press. Overnight, the Ranger hex was Topic A. No wonder. Greg Adams, the Canucks' secret weapon, won it with barely 30 seconds left in the first overtime. McLean had made 52 saves to carry the Canucks into their first-ever games in June.

"I've never seen a goalie put on a display like that in my life," Trevor Linden would say months later, remembering as if it were yesterday. "Never."

Game 2: June 2, 1994. Madison Square Garden, New York.

Rangers 3–1. The Rangers won the next three games, as we know. The Canucks were never really in the game. They did hit three cross-bars. They only lost it when Mike Richter made pointblank saves off Martin Gelinas and then the Canucks gave up an empty-netter with McLean out.

Game 3: June 4, 1994. Pacific Coliseum, Vancouver.

Rangers 5–1. The expulsion of Pavel Bure with the score 1–1, and Glenn Anderson's goal less than a minute later, effectively decided the game. Before Bure's high-sticking major, the Canucks had outshot the Rangers 7–1, beaten them up physically, and played their best hockey of the series.

Game 4: June 7, 1994. Pacific Coliseum, Vancouver.

Rangers 4–2. The Canucks dominated the first period of Game 4, leading 2–0 after the first 20 minutes, but then Brian Leetch took over. The lasting image is the overhead photo of Richter stopping Bure's penalty shot, foiling the same move the Russian Rocket had put on Mike Vernon. Still, the Canucks were in it until, with 2:04 left and the score 3-2 for the Rangers, Steve Larmer's long shot was deflected on the way in by Dave Babych, and caught McLean going the other way.

Above: *McLean makes a save off an Alexei Kovalev backhand. Who would be the best Russian in the Stanley Cup? Bure was asked. "Whoever wins…" he answered.* Below: *Mike Richter makes this penalty shot save on Pavel Bure in Game 4 by kicking his pad forward, jamming the puck before Bure can go around him.*

Above: *Craig MacTavish, the last man playing NHL hockey without a helmet, is a target for John McIntyre's attempt to provoke a retaliation penalty.* Below: *Geoff Courtnall and Sergei Zubov. With his stickblade on the ice – forming a tripod with his skates – Courtnall is almost immovable.*

Facing page: *The violent game-within-a-game: Canuck defenceman Jeff Brown jousts with Ranger winger Steve Larmer for position in front of the Vancouver net. Playoff games are often decided in these one-on-one battles.*

Game 5: June 9, 1994. Madison Square Garden, New York.

Canucks 6–3. Afterward, *Hockey Night in Canada* host Ron McLean would call the amazing spectacle that unfolded during the third period of Game 5 at Madison Square Garden "a comeback for the ages." It will forever seem a touch unreal. It was poetic that Babych scored the winning goal, even if it was buried in the barrage of eight goals in 12:38 that turned the game around, and then turned it around again. The Rangers scored the first three of the period to take a 3–1 lead. The Canucks then scored five to run roughshod over the victory celebrations planned for that night in Manhattan. Both Bure and Courtnall scored two.

Former Canuck coach and current *Hockey Night In Canada* colour man Harry Neale would observe during Game 6 that the Stanley Cup "is a slippery trophy, isn't it? And it may be slipping through the hands of the New York Rangers."

"All we wanted to do," Courtnall told Red Fisher, the dean of hockey writers, "was protect the lead we had going into the third period." Yeah, right.

Game 6: June 11, 1994. Pacific Coliseum, Vancouver.

Canucks 4–1. In a Stanley Cup final that had everything, the entire gamut of playoff emotions were somehow intensified and compressed into 43 seconds of nonstop end-to-end action. Agony to ecstasy, joy to despair: The goals that were exchanged between the Canucks and Rangers without a stoppage in play were the series in miniature – with, for one glorious moment, the Canucks as victors.

The Canucks toyed with the Rangers through the first period. They had 15 shots with five minutes left in the frame, and were unlucky to emerge ahead only 1–0. Jeff Brown scored the goal on an armour-piercing point shot that passed over Richter's shoulder.

Then Courtnall made it 2–0 in the second, after Bure carried the puck into the Ranger zone and moved it to Lumme in the slot. Lumme moved it to Courtnall at the crease, and he started across the Ranger goalmouth. The puck hit Ranger Alexei Kovalev's stick and was deflected past Richter as he fell. The goalie reached back to pull out the puck. Too late. Kovalev got retribution two minutes later when his centring pass hit Murray Craven's shinguards and bounced past McLean: 2–1.

The Canucks took a 3–1 lead on a heads-up play by Linden. Mark Messier had been beating Linden on faceoffs 6–0 so far in the game. So, with a faceoff deep in the Ranger end, Linden went forward with

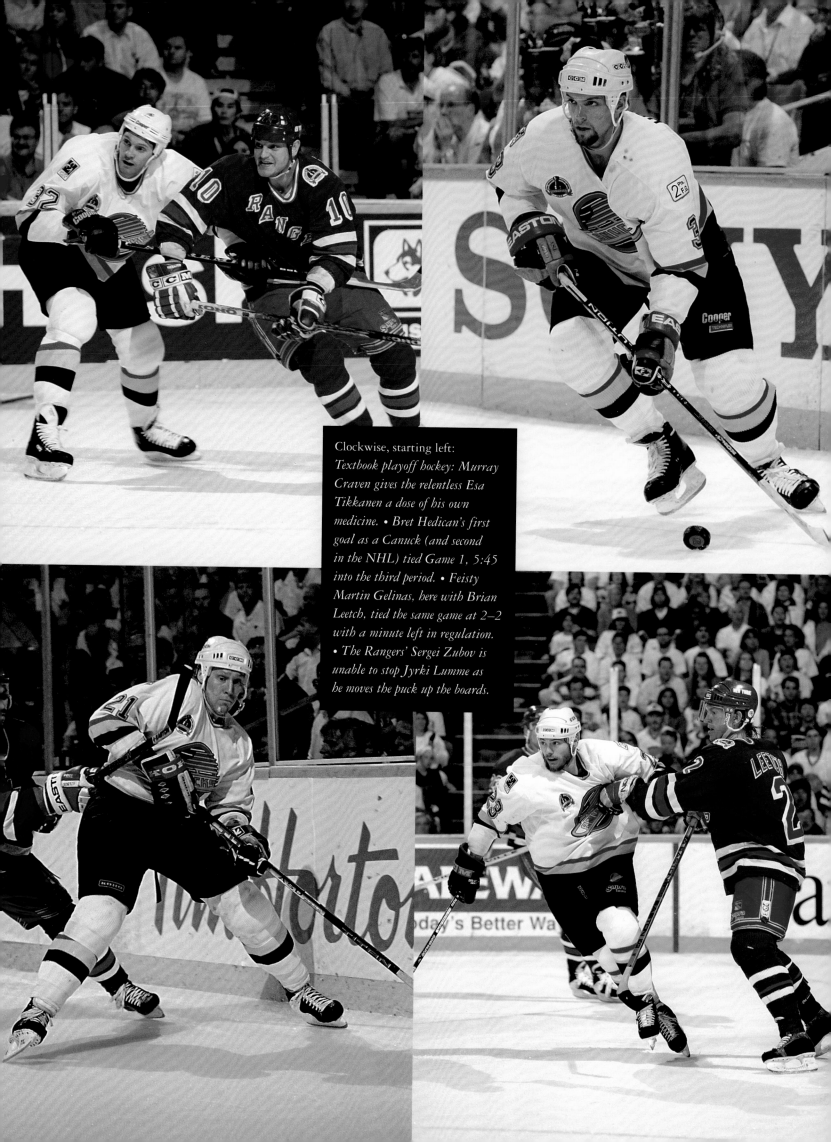

Clockwise, starting left:
Textbook playoff hockey: Murray Craven gives the relentless Esa Tikkanen a dose of his own medicine. • Bret Hedican's first goal as a Canuck (and second in the NHL) tied Game 1, 5:45 into the third period. • Feisty Martin Gelinas, here with Brian Leetch, tied the same game at 2–2 with a minute left in regulation. • The Rangers' Sergei Zubov is unable to stop Jyrki Lumme as he moves the puck up the boards.

Playoff practices are designed to keep players loose. Assistant coach Rick Ley shares a laugh with Cliff Ronning.

Coach Pat Quinn and assistant Stan Smyl together represented 159 games of playoff experience, playing and coaching, going into the 1994 Stanley Cup final.

Canucks assistant coach Ron Smith talks strategy with Pat Quinn.

Following pages: *Although play continued for 43 seconds after the fact, Geoff Courtnall's high backhand shot at 1:34 of the third period of Game 6 was, in fact, the game clincher.*

the puck instead of drawing it back, then beat Messier to it behind the Rangers net. The Canucks captain moved it to the right point, where Jeff Brown one-timed a bazooka blast past Richter at 8:35. A minute later the Coliseum fans were chanting *We Want the Cup.*

The stage was set for a 43-second game-within-a-game minidrama that was wiped off the clock when the ensuing schmozzle was sorted out by the officials, but cannot be erased from human memory. Any number of goals might have been scored during that last gasp all-out offensive by both teams. Only one counted.

With three minutes left, Bure can't quite break away from Ranger defenceman Jay Wells, who knocks him down in the faceoff circle, takes the puck and carries it to centre ice. He slaps a knuckleball that bounces in front of McLean, who does the splits. The puck slides by the left post, missing by inches. The crowd groans as one.

The puck goes to the corner, squirts out of a four-man scrum, and Bret Hedican pushes it down the ice with Bure on a two-on-one. Bure shakes his stick, looking for a pass, but Hedican holds it, refusing to risk an interception and quick turnaround by the Rangers. In close, he hits Richter with his shot. Bure pounces on the rebound, but Richter is there. The Rangers ice it.

With 2:18 remaining after the ensuing faceoff, the Rangers' Kevin Lowe brings the puck through the neutral zone, crosses the Canucks blue line, and feeds Kovalev, who shoots off McLean's glove. Lowe keeps the puck in the Canucks' zone, shoots it into the left corner, and a centring pass hits Cliff Ronning's skate and pops straight up.

Faceoff, 1:53 left. Linden ties up Kovalev, but a Ranger picks up the loose puck at their feet and drills a low shot that McLean stops. The rebound goes to Gerald Diduck, who quickly moves the puck straight ahead to Nathan LaFayette. LaFayette takes the pass in his skates and kicks the puck ahead, but loses his balance. Falling, he hooks the puck past Ranger defenceman Jeff Beukeboom and across the slot. Courtnall, moving toward LaFayette, takes it crossing the goalmouth. Richter, who has moved to his right with the pass, falls as Courtnall moves the other way, and Courtnall backhands the puck just inside the crossbar. The crowd, already wild, picks up the volume. They think Courtnall has scored.

But the noise dies away as the puck falls at the feet of a Ranger defenceman, who moves it past a confused Courtnall to a winger, who turns away. The puck hits his skate. Bure, fresh off the bench, is in full flight. He blasts it wide.

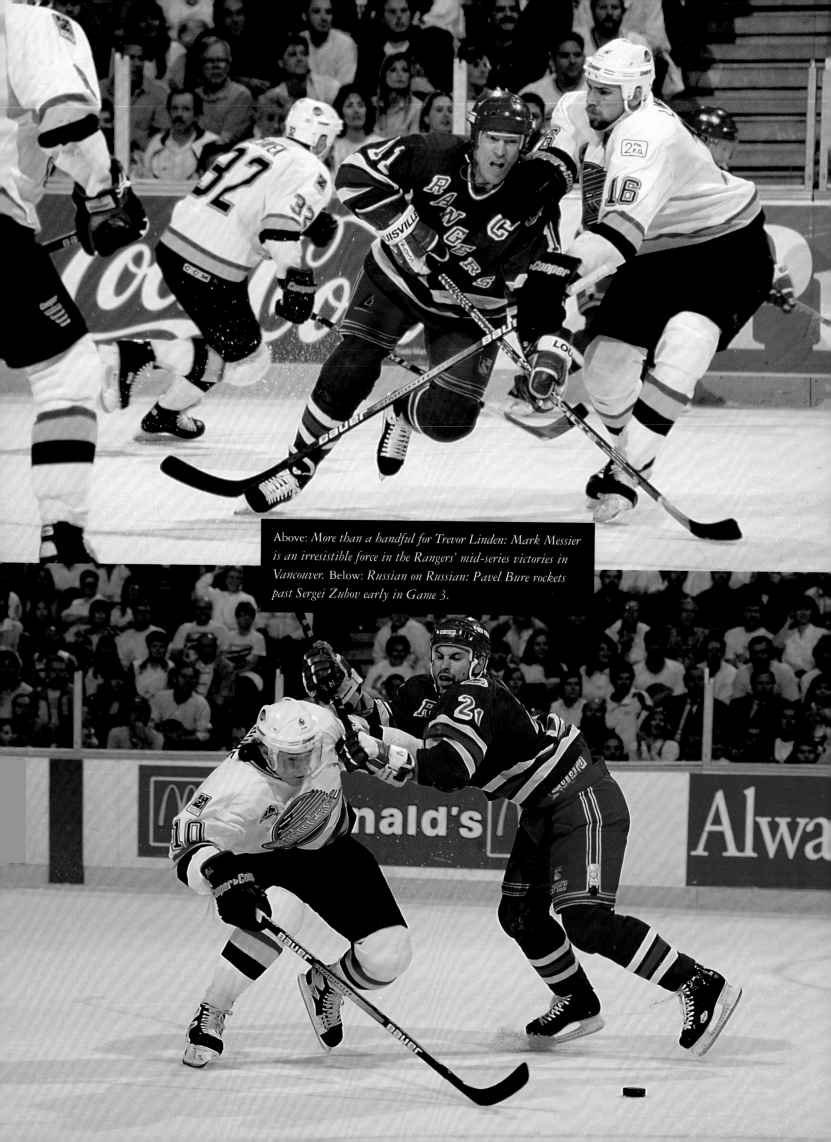

Above: *More than a handful for Trevor Linden: Mark Messier is an irresistible force in the Rangers' mid-series victories in Vancouver.* Below: *Russian on Russian: Pavel Bure rockets past Sergei Zubov early in Game 3.*

In the heat of battle: Kirk McLean and Dave Babych have the near post covered, Mark Messier starts around the Canucks net. Shawn Antoski has Steve Larmer in his sights at the far side.

In Game 6 action, Pavel Bure ignites the Coliseum crowd by making Brian Leetch pay in advance for his four-point night.

Following pages: *Sergio Momesso drives past Doug Lidster to confront Joey Kocur face to face during Game 6 at the Coliseum.*

With a little over 1:10 left on the clock and no stoppage since the Linden-Kovalev faceoff, Brian Leetch gathers up the puck in his own end and starts down the ice. He makes a short pass near the red line to Glenn Anderson, who crosses the Canuck blue line at the far boards and begins one of his trademark dashes around the defence. Denied the outside route, he passes the puck across the Canucks' goalmouth from the corner. Mark Messier taps it in at the right post.

"This is what we've feared forever," exclaims Neale, thinking Courtnall has scored. If his goal counts, it's 4–1 and the Canucks are back to Manhattan in their own seventh heaven. If not, it's 3–2 with a minute left and anything can happen. This moment is what the video replay was invented for. The fans are proven right. Courtnall scores. The subsequent 43 seconds are erased from the clock. The series goes seven games. Arthur Griffiths calls Game 6 the best game ever played at the Coliseum.

Game 7: June 14, 1994. Madison Square Garden, New York. Rangers 3–2. This game was a highlight for Kirk McLean, "even though we lost." It was a magnificent game, fully as exciting as the one that preceded it. *The Globe and Mail* gave it a five-star rating and called it "a breakthrough for the sport of hockey." *Sports Illustrated* wondered, for once, if hockey wasn't outmarketing basketball. Most people in Vancouver remember where they watched it on television.

It was one of those games to be proud of having played in. There had been only 10 seventh games in the 56 Stanley Cup finals since 1939. The day before, Rangers goalie Mike Richter said he would like it never to end. He knew it had to, but he was in no rush to get it over with.

Consider this. Ron Smith, the man who saw the way clear through to the finals in 1982 after the Canucks beat Calgary in that year's preliminary series, thinks that one less day of rest between Games 6 and 7 would have made all the difference for the Canucks:

"Give the Rangers credit. If there was one game that would have shaken the Rangers up, that [Game 5] was it. Just when you thought they were going to score nine goals on us we did it to them. And I guess it did [shake them up], because we blasted them in the next one."

Left: *The toll of "the most exciting game ever played at the Pacific Coliseum" shows on the faces of Trevor Linden and Kirk McLean.* Above: *The Canucks and their fans celebrate the 4–1 win that forced a seventh and deciding Stanley Cup game for only the 10th time since 1939.*

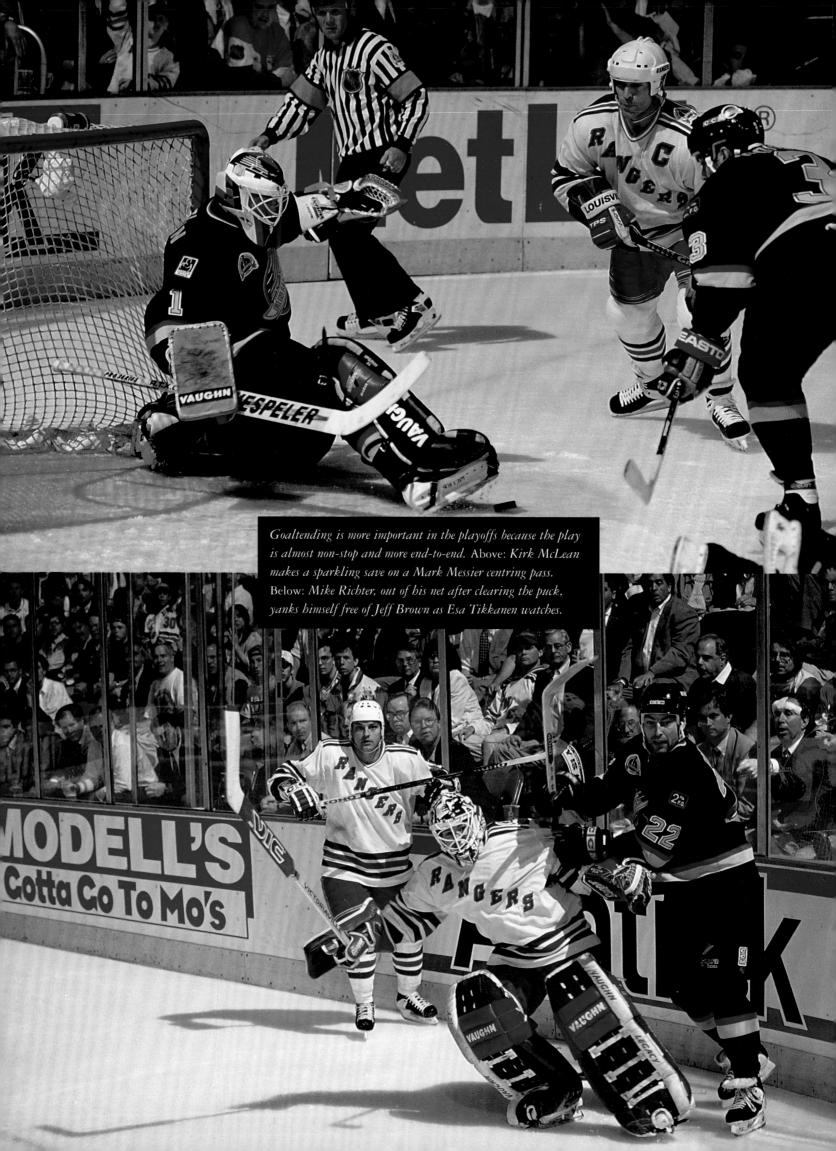

Goaltending is more important in the playoffs because the play is almost non-stop and more end-to-end. Above: Kirk McLean makes a sparkling save on a Mark Messier centring pass. Below: Mike Richter, out of his net after clearing the puck, yanks himself free of Jeff Brown as Esa Tikkanen watches.

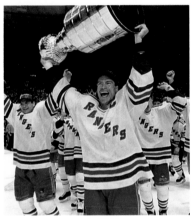

A drought of 54 years came to an end for Ranger fans as the curse was laid to rest with their 1994 Stanley Cup victory. Playoff MVP Brian Leetch (top) and Ranger captain Mark Messier (bottom) must have enjoyed the New York fans' sense of humour, as a sign posted high in Madison Square Garden in Game 7 read "Now I can die in peace."

But it didn't work out that way. Some people are still waiting for Nathan LaFayette to score. With barely more than a minute left, the New Westminster native hit the Ranger goalpost with a loud ping! that still reverberates from coast to coast. He was surprised to find a perfect pass from Courtnall on his stick, one-timed it, hit the post dead-on and was mauled as the puck came back to him. He has been reliving the moment ever since.

The Rangers had to prove they were good enough, and the Canucks made them prove it. Giving the Rangers their due only underlines the Canucks' achievement. Brian Leetch was a worthy Conn Smythe Trophy winner as Most Valuable Player of the playoffs.

Kirk McLean was left with that miserable feeling that only the losing goalie in a big game knows. "I was remembering the feeling of losing" – soaking in it, replaying every goal – "and watching them celebrate. For five minutes we sat on the bench and wondered What's going on? It's the biggest memory because it's the last thing that happened."

"You work that hard for seven games," Geoff Courtnall told *Sun* hockey writer Iain MacIntyre, "and then you see the other team jumping up and down and celebrating. It's probably the hardest thing to take. We came together as a team and thought we could do it. It just would have been nice to have something to go home with."

Take this home: If asked to pick one of the Stanley Cup finalists to coach for the next five years, the choice would be clear: The Canucks. "Absolutely," says the man who will have that opportunity, the Canucks' new head coach, Rick Ley. "The Canucks have an opportunity to be a good team for many years to come. Our impact players are still very young. With the Rangers, their impact players are all older, at or past their peaks."

There's not far to go. Just one more step.

When Pat Quinn became general manager of the Vancouver NHL club in May 1987, he was presented with a replica of his old number 3 white-with-blue-and-green trim Canucks jersey by the Canadian Press's veteran hockey writer, Grant Kerr. Quinn kept it hanging in his office as a reminder of how far he had come in hockey, and — as baseball manager Whitey Herzog once put it — how good the game has been to him since he stopped trying to play it.

That isn't all the jersey meant. It announced a hockey club that had been around long enough to develop management talent. There was a Vancouver Canuck tradition, and it was worth celebrating. Arriving at that stage is a milestone for any institution.

Funny thing, when tradition becomes important, the future emerges with astonishing clarity. As the Canucks begin their 25th season, they show signs of becoming something more than just Vancouver's major-league team, and more than being a fast-growing subsidiary of a media and entertainment empire. The club is becoming a citizen of the city on its own account.

Playoff runs such as the Canucks' 1982 and 1994 Stanley Cup final drives do a lot to cement the bonds between the town and its team. They get the whole town talking about one topic. The moods of a million and a half people rise and fall in unison. Anyone with a connection to the team becomes a celebrity. Pavel Bure's hairdresser finds himself being interviewed by reporters.

The winning spirit radiates out like the ripples from a penny in a wishing-well, and the entire province gets drawn into the widening reflections.

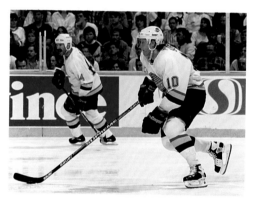

The future burns even brighter for the Canucks with "The Russian Rocket" signed to a long term contract.

The move downtown in 1995 will make the hockey club part of the city in a way it never was in the nowhereland of the Pacific National Exhibition. General Motors Place, set between the inbound and outbound roadways of the Georgia Viaduct, will soon be what Maple Leaf Gardens and the Forum are for Toronto and Montreal.

Within 10 years, the new home of the Canucks will be in the midst of the most vital inner-city neighbourhood in the country, with tens of thousands of fans within easy walking distance. Watch the *Hockey Night in Canada* opening montage closely next time. It is an abstract but recognizably urban motif with lights whizzing along some fast track toward the highrise canyons downtown. That is exactly what General Motors Place will be.

General Motors Place will be a sensational building at night — it will light up its surroundings and draw people to it. Conceptually, it will consist of a transparent drum, with square corners of steel and concrete to recall the area's industrial past. Events inside will be glimpsed from the viaducts through glazed walls, with impressions augmented by video screens, lights and signage.

The building is not round but elliptical, so the seats will conform better than those of the Pacific Coliseum to the shape of the rink. Sightlines will be much better, especially high on each side of the centre red line. The sound system will be 25 years better, the scoreboard will include big-scale video replays, and even the shut-in fan who Jim Robson always thinks of will benefit from BC Tel's state-of-the-art broadcast hook-ups. A big difference the fans will notice will be the lack of line-ups between periods.

Tom Anselmi, General Motors Place's Vice President of Operations, promises better food and drink service, and, "no lineups to the washrooms."

"Not even for the women's washrooms?"

"Not even there. Five times the number of washrooms as the Coliseum."

A staggering claim to make. There will actually be more women's than men's washrooms. Amazing – the architects have studied actual crowd behaviour and requirements in designing General Motors Place.

In contrast to the fibre-optic, plugged-in arena the Canucks will soon call home, another part of the hockey

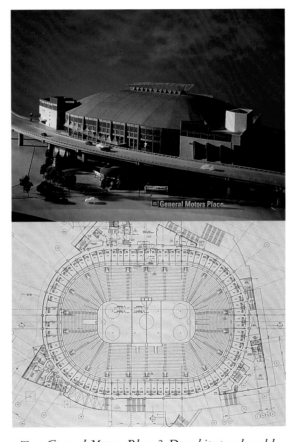

Top: *General Motors Place 3-D architectural model.*
Bottom: *Blueprint overhead view of arena seating.*

club's future resides in a mansion built in 1910. Glen Brae, "one of the most unforgettable of Shaughnessey homes," as architectural historian Harold Kalman writes in *Exploring Vancouver*, is the wonderful twin-turreted, shingled home that is being renovated into North America's first freestanding hospice for terminally ill children, which will open in 1995. It will be called Canuck Place.

How is it that the greatest needs so often go unaddressed for so long? Brenda Eng, an energetic nurse at B.C.'s Children's Hospital, has confronted that question every working day. Her experience working at Helen House, a children's hospice in Britain, inspired her to seek support for a similar facility in British Columbia. Doing something about it seemed impossible until she was introduced to the Canuck Foundation, the community services arm of the Vancouver Canucks, which in the past had assisted organizations like Ronald McDonald House, the Boys and Girls Club of Greater Vancouver, B.C.'s Children's Hospital and the CKNW Orphans Fund. Founded by Arthur Griffiths and his wife, Joanne, with a mandate to assist children, the Canuck Foundation has committed to raise money to help build and operate Canuck Place.

"When we were presented the idea for Canuck Place, it seemed a natural fit for what we had been doing with the Foundation," says Canuck Foundation president Joanne Griffiths. "Since we have become involved, we have been overwhelmed by the support of corporate partners, different levels of government and the generous donations of thousands of individual British Columbians. It is inspiring to be part of this."

Canuck player appearances and events organized by their wives have also inspired wide participation and a generous response. But there is a closer link between the kids who will benefit from Canuck Place and the athletes.

"The kids are what heroes are made of," says Brenda Eng, "and so are the players. The players are a symbol of health and team spirit. They [players and sick children] have common ground. Even when your body is giving out, you can still hope. You can still watch the game."

As a hospice, Canuck Place is intended to offer "care that begins when there is no cure." In the home-like family environment, the hospice will provide direct care for the children and give their families a break from the strain of caring for them. Grief support programs will also be provided for the families.

Canuck Place past honourary spokesperson Trevor Linden shares a special hug with Bryce.

The hockey club's involvement with Canuck Place helps put everything else it does in the community into perspective. But the values that go into the hockey operation can be as positive and human as the social commitments.

One of the differences in management style that Pat Quinn brought to the club was patience and a willingness to be loyal to people. Six years ago, when he agreed to be Quinn's assistant, Brian Burke was a player agent, a very bright one. Now he is a vice-president of the NHL. In a smaller way, it could be said that a Martin Gelinas, say, or a Tim Hunter has had his worth enhanced by his time with the Canucks. This is a priceless reputation for any organization, let alone a major-league sports franchise. In line with the idea of recognizing a player's contribution instead of retiring him and losing everything he has learned, the Canucks are routinely promoting from within.

Who better to instill the will to overachieve in young players than Stan Smyl, an assistant coach with the Canucks since he retired in 1991? Who better to find European talent than the greatest European talent the Canucks had until Pavel Bure, Thomas Gradin? Who better to teach the value of toughness and heads-up play to the farmhands in Syracuse than the newly appointed Curt Fraser? There you have it: the best forward line in Vancouver's 25 years, reunited within the club's far-flung organization.

Glen Hanlon was the most self-analytical of goaltenders. Who better to coach the most technically proficient of goaltenders, Kirk McLean? Suddenly, the Canucks are one of the rare NHL clubs with depth at the most important position.

Jack McIlhargey, a lifelong Burnaby resident, is head coach at Syracuse (where the Canucks' top developmental team has been moved from Hamilton and renamed the Crunch). Steve Tambellini, from one of Trail's great hockey families, is director of media and public relations. Ron Delorme, an insider's hero of the 1982 playoff run, is the club's western scout.

One effect of honouring people's contributions is to create a kind of talent surplus. To have been associated with the Canucks has more worth in the marketplace. We see ex-Canucks becoming NHL coaches elsewhere: Marc Crawford with the Quebec Nordiques and Colin Campbell with the New York Rangers.

There is a retroactive aspect to all of this. In honouring

Top: *Steve Tambellini,*
Canuck centreman, 1985–86 to 1987–88.
Bottom: *Jack McIlhargey,*
Canucks defenceman, 1976–77 to 1979–80

the Vancouver Canuck tradition as Pat Quinn did by hanging his replica jersey in his office, men who played for the team 20 years ago are made to feel a little prouder. Recently the Canucks Alumni Association was recognized by the league as a model for other NHL teams to emulate.

Of course, it helps that the man in charge of the big-league organization, Pat Quinn, is a member of the association, as well.

Regardless of what the football coach said, winning is neither the most important thing nor the only thing. It is an outcome, not a birthright or a state of being. It has to be earned every day. It results from doing the small, everyday tasks in life as well as possible, and by treating the people around you as well as possible.

One thing everyone understands about winning is that it makes other good things possible. The Vancouver Canucks have certainly proven that and, as they begin their silver anniversary season, the future of NHL hockey has never been brighter.

After having come so close to winning the Stanley Cup, the 1993–94 Canucks have created a new standard of excellence for themselves.

And for their fans.

1970–71
Season Finish – 6th in East Division

GP	W	L	T	GF	GA	PTS	PCT
78	24	46	8	229	296	56	.359

Coach: Hal Laycoe • GM: Norman Robert Poile
Captain: Orland Kurtenbach

TOP TEN SCORERS	GP	G	A	PTS	PIM
Andre Boudrias	77	25	41	66	16
Wayne Maki	78	25	38	63	99
Rosaire Paiement	78	34	28	62	152
Murray Hall	77	21	38	59	22
Dale Tallon	78	14	42	56	58
Orland Kurtenbach	52	21	32	53	84
Mike Corrigan	76	21	28	49	103
Ray Cullen	70	12	21	33	42
Poul Popiel	78	10	22	32	61
Ted Taylor	56	11	16	27	53

THE GOALIES	GP	AVE	SO	RECORD
George Gardner	18	3.38	0	6-8-1
Charlie Hodge	35	3.41	0	15-13-5
Dunc Wilson	35	4.28	0	3-25-2

1971–72
Season Finish – 7th in East Division

GP	W	L	T	GF	GA	PTS	PCT
78	20	50	8	203	297	48	.308

Coach: Hal Laycoe • GM: Norman Robert Poile
Captain: Orland Kurtenbach

TOP TEN SCORERS	GP	G	A	PTS	PIM
Andre Boudrias	78	27	34	61	24
Orland Kurtenbach	78	24	37	51	48
Jocelyn Guevremont	75	13	38	51	44
Dave Balon	75	23	24	47	23
Wayne Maki	76	22	25	47	43
Wayne Connelly	68	19	25	44	14
Dale Tallon	69	17	27	44	78
Rosaire Paiement	69	10	19	29	117
Dennis Kearns	73	3	26	29	59
Bobby Schmautz	60	12	13	25	82

THE GOALIES	GP	AVE	SO	RECORD
Dunc Wilson	53	3.61	1	16-30-3
Ed Dyck	12	3.66	0	1-6-2
George Gardner	24	4.17	0	3-14-3

1972–73
Season Finish – 7th in East Division

GP	W	L	T	GF	GA	PTS	PCT
78	22	47	9	233	339	51	.340

Coach: Vic Stasluk • GM: Norman Robert Poile
Captain: Orland Kurtenbach

TOP TEN SCORERS	GP	G	A	PTS	PIM
Bobby Schmautz	77	38	33	71	137
Andre Boudrias	77	30	40	70	24
Richard Lemieux	78	17	35	52	41
Bobby Lalonde	77	20	27	47	32
Don Tannahil	78	22	21	43	21
Jocelyn Guevremont	78	16	26	42	46
Don Lever	78	12	26	38	49
Dale Tallon	75	13	24	37	83
John Wright	71	10	27	37	37
Dennis Kearns	72	4	33	37	51

THE GOALIES	GP	AVE	SO	RECORD
Dunc Wilson	43	3.94	1	13-21-5
Ed Dyck	25	4.53	1	5-17-1
Bruce Bullock	14	4.79	0	3-8-3
Dave McLelland	2	5.00	0	1-1-0

1973–74
Season Finish – 7th in East Division

GP	W	L	T	GF	GA	PTS	PCT
78	24	43	11	224	296	59	.378

Coach: Bill McCreary, Phil Maloney
GM: Hal Laycoe • Captain: Orland Kurtenbach

TOP TEN SCORERS	GP	G	A	PTS	PIM
Andre Boudrias	78	16	59	75	18
Dennis Ververgaert	78	26	31	57	25
Don Lever	78	23	25	48	28
Gerry O'Flaherty	78	22	20	42	18
Jocelyn Guevremont	72	15	24	39	34
Dave Dunn	68	11	22	33	76
Barry Wilkins	78	3	28	31	123
Chris Oddleifson	70	13	16	29	44
John Gould	75	13	12	25	10
Paulin Bordeleau	68	11	13	24	20

THE GOALIES	GP	AVE	SO	RECORD
Gary Smith	66	3.44	3	20-33-8
Ed Dyck	12	4.63	0	2-5-2
Jacques Caron	10	4.90	0	2-5-1

1974–75
Season Finish – 1st in Smythe Division

GP	W	L	T	GF	GA	PTS	PCT
80	38	32	10	271	254	86	.538

Coach: Phil Maloney • GM: Phil Maloney
Captain: no captain

TOP TEN SCORERS	GP	G	A	PTS	PIM
Andre Boudrias	77	16	62	78	46
Don Lever	80	38	30	68	49
John Gould	78	34	31	65	27
Dennis Ververgaert	57	19	32	51	25
Chris Oddleifson	60	16	35	51	54
Paulin Bordeleau	67	17	31	48	21
Bob Dailey	70	12	36	48	103
Bobby Lalonde	74	17	30	47	48
Gerry O'Flaherty	80	25	17	42	37
Garry Monahan	79	14	20	34	51

THE GOALIES	GP	AVE	SO	RECORD
Gary Smith	72	3.09	6	32-24-9
Ken Lockett	25	3.16	2	6-7-1
Bruce Bullock	1	4.00	0	0-1-0

1975–76
Season Finish – 2nd in Smythe Division

GP	W	L	T	GF	GA	PTS	PCT
80	33	32	15	271	272	81	.506

Coach: Phil Maloney • GM: Phil Maloney
Captain: Andre Boudrias

TOP TEN SCORERS	GP	G	A	PTS	PIM
Dennis Ververgaert	80	37	34	71	53
Don Lever	80	25	40	65	93
Chris Oddleifson	80	16	46	62	88
John Gould	70	32	27	59	16
Rick Blight	74	25	31	56	29
Dennis Kearns	80	5	46	51	48
Bobby Lalonde	71	14	36	50	46
Bob Dailey	67	15	24	39	119
Gerry O'Flaherty	68	20	18	38	47
Andre Boudrias	71	7	31	38	10

THE GOALIES	GP	AVE	SO	RECORD
Curt Ridley	9	2.28	1	6-0-2
Ken Lockett	30	3.47	0	7-8-7
Gary Smith	51	3.50	2	20-24-6

1976–77
Season Finish – 4th in Smythe Division

GP	W	L	T	GF	GA	PTS	PCT
80	25	42	13	235	294	63	.394

Coach: Phil Maloney, Orland Kurtenbach
GM: Phil Maloney • Captain: Chris Oddleifson

TOP TEN SCORERS	GP	G	A	PTS	PIM
Rick Blight	78	28	40	68	32
Dennis Kearns	80	5	55	60	60
Don Lever	80	27	30	57	28
Dennis Ververgaert	79	27	18	45	38
Garry Monahan	76	18	26	44	48
Hilliard Graves	79	18	25	43	34
Chris Oddleifson	80	14	26	40	81
Ron Sedlbauer	70	18	20	38	29
Derek Sanderson	48	15	22	37	56
Bobby Lalonde	68	17	15	32	39

THE GOALIES	GP	AVE	SO	RECORD
Cesare Maniago	47	3.36	1	17-21-9
Curt Ridley	37	3.88	0	8-21-4
Bruce Bullock	1	6.67	0	0-0-0

1977–78
Season Finish – 3rd in Smythe Division

GP	W	L	T	GF	GA	PTS	PCT
80	20	43	17	239	320	57	.356

Coach: Orland Kurtenbach • GM: Jake Milford
Captain: Don Lever

TOP TEN SCORERS	GP	G	A	PTS	PIM
Mike Walton	65	29	37	66	30
Rick Blight	80	25	38	63	33
Dennis Ververgaert	80	21	33	54	23
Don Lever	75	17	32	49	58
Pit Martin	64	16	32	48	36
Hilliard Graves	80	21	26	47	18
Dennis Kearns	80	4	43	47	27
Jere Gillis	79	23	18	41	35
Chris Oddleifson	78	17	22	39	64
Ron Sedlbauer	62	18	12	30	25

THE GOALIES	GP	AVE	SO	RECORD
Murray Bannerman	1	0.00	0	0-0-0
Glen Hanlon	4	2.70	0	1-2-1
Cesare Maniago	46	4.02	1	10-24-8
Curt Ridley	40	4.06	0	9-17-8

Statistical information provided by the Vancouver Canucks.

1978–79
Season Finish – 2nd in Smythe Division

GP	W	L	T	GF	GA	PTS	PCT
80	25	42	13	217	291	63	.394

Coach: Harry Neale • GM: Jake Milford
Captain: Don Lever • Kevin McCarthy

TOP TEN SCORERS	GP	G	A	PTS	PIM
Ron Sedlbauer	79	40	16	56	26
Thomas Gradin	76	20	31	51	22
Don Lever	71	23	21	44	17
Stan Smyl	62	14	24	38	89
Chris Oddleifson	67	11	26	37	51
Curt Fraser	78	16	19	35	116
Dennis Kearns	78	3	31	34	28
Harold Snepsts	76	7	24	31	130
Pit Martin	64	12	14	26	24
Hilliard Graves	62	11	15	26	14

THE GOALIES	GP	AVE	SO	RECORD
Glen Hanlon	31	3.10	3	12-13-5
Gary Bromley	38	3.81	2	11-19-6
Dunc Wilson	17	4.17	0	2-10-2

1979–80
Season Finish – 3rd in Smythe Division

GP	W	L	T	GF	GA	PTS	PCT
80	27	37	16	256	281	70	.481

Coach: Harry Neale • GM: Jake Milford
Captain: Kevin McCarthy

TOP TEN SCORERS	GP	G	A	PTS	PIM
Stan Smyl	77	31	47	78	204
Thomas Gradin	80	30	45	75	22
Ivan Boldirev	79	32	35	67	34
Dave Williams	78	30	23	53	278
Kevin McCarthy	79	15	30	45	70
Curt Fraser	78	17	25	42	143
Lars Lindgren	73	5	30	35	66
Per-Olov Brasar	70	10	24	34	7
Jere Gillis	67	13	17	30	108
Darcy Rota	70	15	14	29	78

THE GOALIES	GP	AVE	SO	RECORD
Gary Bromley	15	3.00	1	8-2-4
Glen Hanlon	57	3.47	0	17-29-10
Curt Ridley	10	3.91	0	2-6-2

1980–81
Season Finish – 3rd in Smythe Division

GP	W	L	T	GF	GA	PTS	PCT
80	28	32	20	289	301	76	.475

Coach: Harry Neale • GM: Jake Milford
Captain: Kevin McCarthy

TOP TEN SCORERS	GP	G	A	PTS	PIM
Thomas Gradin	79	21	48	69	34
Stan Smyl	80	25	38	63	171
Per-Olov Brasar	80	22	41	63	8
Dave Williams	77	35	27	62	343
Bobby Schmautz	73	27	34	61	137
Ivan Boldirev	72	26	33	59	34
Blair MacDonald	63	24	33	57	37
Darcy Rota	80	25	31	56	124
Kevin McCarthy	80	16	37	53	85
Curt Fraser	77	25	24	49	118

THE GOALIES	GP	AVE	SO	RECORD
Richard Brodeur	52	3.51	0	17-18-16
Gary Bromley	20	3.80	0	6-6-4
Glen Hanlon	17	4.44	1	5-8-0

1981–82
Season Finish – 2nd in Smythe Division

GP	W	L	T	GF	GA	PTS	PCT
80	30	33	17	290	286	77	.481

Coach: Harry Neale, Roger Neilson
GM: Jake Milford • Captain: Kevin McCarthy

TOP TEN SCORERS	GP	G	A	PTS	PIM
Thomas Gradin	76	37	49	86	32
Stan Smyl	80	34	44	78	144
Ivan Boldirev	78	33	40	73	45
Curt Fraser	79	28	39	67	175
Ivan Hlinka	72	23	37	60	16
Tony Currie	60	23	25	48	19
Lars Molin	72	15	31	46	10
Kevin McCarthy	71	6	39	45	84
Darcy Rota	51	20	20	40	139
Dave Williams	77	17	21	38	341

THE GOALIES	GP	AVE	SO	RECORD
Rick Heinz	3	3.00	1	2-1-0
Richard Brodeur	52	3.35	2	20-18-12
Glen Hanlon	28	3.95	1	8-14-5

1982–83
Season Finish – 3rd in Smythe Division

GP	W	L	T	GF	GA	PTS	PCT
80	30	35	15	303	309	75	.469

Coach: Roger Neilson • GM: Harry Neale
Captain: Stan Smyl

TOP TEN SCORERS	GP	G	A	PTS	PIM
Stan Smyl	74	38	50	88	114
Thomas Gradin	80	32	54	86	61
Darcy Rota	73	42	39	81	88
Ivan Hlinka	65	19	44	63	12
Doug Halward	75	19	33	52	83
Rick Lanz	74	10	38	48	46
Patrik Sundstrom	74	23	23	46	30
Kevin McCarthy	74	12	28	40	88
Lars Molin	58	12	27	39	23
Jiri Bubla	72	2	28	30	59

THE GOALIES	GP	AVE	SO	RECORD
John Garrett	17	3.08	1	7-6-3
Richard Brodeur	58	3.79	0	21-26-8
Ken Ellacott	12	4.43	0	2-3-4
Frank Caprice	1	9.09	0	0-0-0

1983–84
Season Finish – 3rd in Smythe Division

GP	W	L	T	GF	GA	PTS	PCT
80	32	39	9	306	328	73	.456

Coach: Roger Neilson, Harry Neale
GM: Harry Neale • Captain: Stan Smyl

TOP TEN SCORERS	GP	G	A	PTS	PIM
Patrik Sundstrom	78	38	53	91	37
Tony Tanti	79	45	41	86	50
Thomas Gradin	75	21	57	78	32
Stan Smyl	80	24	43	67	136
Rick Lanz	79	18	39	57	45
Darcy Rota	59	28	20	48	73
Gary Lupul	69	17	27	44	51
Jiri Bubla	62	6	33	39	43
Peter McNab	65	15	22	37	20
Cam Neely	56	16	15	31	57

THE GOALIES	GP	AVE	SO	RECORD
Frank Caprice	19	3.39	1	8-8-2
Richard Brodeur	36	4.01	1	10-21-5
John Garrett	29	4.10	0	14-10-2

1984–85
Season Finish – 5th in Smythe Division

GP	W	L	T	GF	GA	PTS	PCT
80	25	46	9	284	401	59	.369

Coach: Bill Laforge • Harry Neale
GM: Harry Neale • Captain: Stan Smyl

TOP TEN SCORERS	GP	G	A	PTS	PIM
Patrik Sundstrom	71	25	43	68	46
Stan Smyl	80	27	37	64	100
Thomas Gradin	76	22	42	64	43
Tony Tanti	68	39	20	59	45
Moe Lemay	74	21	31	52	68
Peter McNab	75	23	25	48	10
Cam Neely	72	21	18	39	137
Petri Skriko	72	21	14	35	10
Al MacAdam	80	14	20	34	27
Doug Halward	71	7	27	34	82

THE GOALIES	GP	AVE	SO	RECORD
Richard Brodeur	51	4.67	0	16-27-6
Frank Caprice	28	4.81	0	8-14-3
John Garrett	10	6.49	0	1-5-0

1985–86
Season Finish – 4th in Smythe Division

GP	W	L	T	GF	GA	PTS	PCT
80	23	44	13	282	333	59	.369

Coach: Tom Watt • GM: Jack Gordon
Captain: Stan Smyl

TOP TEN SCORERS	GP	G	A	PTS	PIM
Petri Skriko	80	38	40	78	34
Tony Tanti	77	39	33	72	85
Patrik Sundstrom	79	18	48	66	28
Stan Smyl	73	27	35	62	144
Rick Lanz	75	15	38	53	73
Thomas Gradin	71	14	27	41	34
Cam Neely	73	14	20	34	126
Doug Halward	70	8	25	33	111
Moe Lemay	48	16	15	31	92
Brent Peterson	77	8	23	31	94

THE GOALIES	GP	AVE	SO	RECORD
Wendell Young	22	3.58	0	4-9-3
Richard Brodeur	64	4.07	2	19-32-8
Frank Caprice	7	5.46	0	0-3-2

1986–87

Season Finish – 5th in Smythe Division

GP	W	L	T	GF	GA	PTS	PCT
80	29	43	8	282	314	66	.413

Coach: Tom Watt • GM: Jack Gordon
Captain: Stan Smyl

TOP TEN SCORERS	GP	G	A	PTS	PIM
Tony Tanti	77	41	38	79	84
Barry Pederson	79	24	52	76	50
Petri Skriko	76	33	41	74	44
Patrik Sundstrom	72	29	42	71	40
Doug Lidster	80	12	51	63	40
Stan Smyl	66	20	23	43	84
Rich Sutter	74	20	22	42	113
Steve Tambellini	72	16	20	36	14
Jim Sandlak	78	15	21	36	66
Raimo Summanen	58	14	11	25	15

THE GOALIES	GP	AVE	SO	RECORD
Richard Brodeur	53	3.59	1	20-25-5
Frank Caprice	25	3.84	0	8-11-2
Troy Gamble	1	4.00	0	0-1-0
Wendell Young	8	5.00	0	1-6-1

1987–88

Season Finish – 5th in Smythe Division

GP	W	L	T	GF	GA	PTS	PCT
80	25	46	9	272	320	59	.368

Coach: Bob McCammon • GM: Pat Quinn
Captain: Stan Smyl

TOP TEN SCORERS	GP	G	A	PTS	PIM
Tony Tanti	73	40	37	77	90
Greg Adams	80	36	40	76	30
Barry Pederson	76	19	52	71	92
Petri Skriko	73	30	34	64	32
Stan Smyl	57	12	25	37	110
Doug Lidster	64	4	32	36	105
Jim Benning	77	7	26	33	58
Jim Sandlak	49	16	15	31	81
Rich Sutter	80	15	15	30	165
Doug Wickenheiser	80	7	19	26	36

THE GOALIES	GP	AVE	SO	RECORD
Steve Weeks	9	3.38	0	4-3-2
Kirk McLean	41	3.71	1	11-27-3
Frank Caprice	22	4.18	0	7-10-2
Richard Brodeur	11	4.39	0	3-6-2

1988–89

Season Finish – 5th in Smythe Division

GP	W	L	T	GF	GA	PTS	PCT
80	33	39	8	251	253	74	.462

Coach: Bob McCammon • GM: Pat Quinn
Captain: Stan Smyl

TOP TEN SCORERS	GP	G	A	PTS	PIM
Petri Skriko	74	30	36	66	57
Trevor Linden	80	30	29	59	41
Paul Reinhart	64	7	50	57	44
Tony Tanti	77	24	25	49	69
Brian Bradley	71	18	27	45	42
Barry Pederson	62	15	26	41	22
Robert Nordmark	80	6	35	41	97
Jim Sandlak	72	20	20	40	99
Steve Bozek	71	17	18	35	64
Greg Adams	61	19	14	33	24

THE GOALIES	GP	AVE	SO	RECORD
Troy Gamble	5	2.38	0	2-3-0
Steve Weeks	35	2.98	0	11-19-5
Kirk McLean	42	3.08	4	20-17-3

1989–90

Season Finish – 5th in Smythe Division

GP	W	L	T	GF	GA	PTS	PCT
80	25	41	14	245	306	64	.400

Coach: Bob McCammon • GM: Pat Quinn
Captain: Stan Smyl

TOP TEN SCORERS	GP	G	A	PTS	PIM
Dan Quinn	78	25	38	63	49
Paul Reinhart	67	17	40	57	30
Trevor Linden	73	21	30	51	43
Greg Adams	65	30	20	50	18
Brian Bradley	67	19	29	48	65
Petri Skriko	77	15	33	48	36
Igor Larionov	74	17	27	44	20
Doug Lidster	80	8	28	36	36
Vladimir Krutov	61	11	23	34	20
Jyrki Lumme	65	4	26	30	49

THE GOALIES	GP	AVE	SO	RECORD
Kirk McLean	63	3.47	0	21-30-10
Steve Weeks	21	4.15	0	4-11-4

1990–91

Season Finish – 4th in Smythe Division

GP	W	L	T	GF	GA	PTS	PCT
80	28	43	9	243	315	65	.410

Coach: Bob McCammon, Pat Quinn
GM: Pat Quinn • Captain: Dan Quinn,
Doug Lidster, Trevor Linden

TOP TEN SCORERS	GP	G	A	PTS	PIM
Trevor Linden	80	33	37	70	65
Geoff Courtnall	77	33	32	65	64
Greg Adams	55	21	24	45	10
Cliff Ronning	59	20	24	44	10
Dave Capuano	61	13	31	44	42
Doug Lidster	78	6	32	38	77
Sergio Momesso	70	16	20	36	174
Igor Larionov	64	13	21	34	14
Steve Bozek	62	15	17	32	22
Robert Kron	76	12	20	32	21

THE GOALIES	GP	AVE	SO	RECORD
Troy Gamble	47	3.45	1	16-16-6
Kirk McLean	41	3.99	0	10-22-3
Bob Mason	6	4.93	0	2-4-0
Steve McKichan	1	6.00	0	0-0-0
Steve Weeks	1	6.10	0	0-1-0

1991–92

Season Finish – 1st in Smythe Division

GP	W	L	T	GF	GA	PTS	PCT
80	42	26	12	285	250	96	.600

Coach: Pat Quinn • GM: Pat Quinn
Captain: Trevor Linden

TOP TEN SCORERS	GP	G	A	PTS	PIM
Trevor Linden	80	31	44	75	99
Cliff Ronning	80	24	47	71	42
Igor Larionov	72	21	44	65	56
Pavel Bure	65	34	26	60	30
Greg Adams	76	30	27	57	26
Geoff Courtnall	70	23	34	57	118
Jyrki Lumme	75	12	32	44	65
Sergio Momesso	58	20	23	43	198
Jim Sandlak	66	16	24	40	176
Tom Fergus	55	15	23	48	21

THE GOALIES	GP	AVE	SO	RECORD
Kirk McLean	65	2.74	5	38-17-9
Troy Gamble	19	4.34	0	4-9-3

1992–93

Season Finish – 1st in Smythe Division

GP	W	L	T	GF	GA	PTS	PCT
84	46	29	9	346	278	101	.601

Coach: Pat Quinn • GM: Pat Quinn
Captain: Trevor Linden

TOP TEN SCORERS	GP	G	A	PTS	PIM
Pavel Bure	83	60	50	110	69
Cliff Ronning	79	29	56	85	30
Geoff Courtnall	84	31	46	77	167
Murray Craven	77	25	52	77	32
Trevor Linden	84	33	39	72	64
Petr Nedved	84	38	33	71	96
Greg Adams	53	25	31	56	14
Dixon Ward	70	22	30	52	82
Anatoli Semenov	75	12	37	49	32
Jyrki Lumme	74	8	36	44	55

THE GOALIES	GP	AVE	SO	RECORD
Kirk McLean	54	3.39	3	28-21-5
Kay Whitmore	31	3.10	1	18-8-4

1993-94

SEASON FINISH: 2nd in Pacific Division of the Western Conference. PLAYOFFS: Defeated the Calgary Flames four games to three, the Dallas Stars four games to one and the Toronto Maple Leafs four games to one before losing the Stanley Cup Finals four games to three to the New York Rangers. Coach and GM: Pat Quinn • Captain: Trevor Linden

REGULAR SEASON

GP	W	L	T	GF	GA	PTS	PCT
84	41	40	3	279	276	85	.506

SCORING	GP	G	A	PTS	PIM
Pavel Bure	76	60	47	107	86
Geoff Courtnall	82	26	44	70	123
Cliff Ronning	76	25	43	68	42
Jeff Brown	74	14	52	66	56
Trevor Linden	84	32	29	61	73
Murray Craven	78	15	40	55	30
Jyrki Lumme	83	13	42	55	50
Jiri Slegr	78	5	33	38	86
Greg Adams	68	13	24	37	20
Dave Babych	73	4	28	32	52
Gino Odjick	76	16	13	29	271
Jimmy Carson	59	11	17	28	24
Martin Gelinas	64	14	14	28	34
Sergio Momesso	68	14	13	27	149
Dana Murzyn	80	6	14	20	109
Brian Glynn	64	2	13	15	53
Joe Charbonneau	30	7	7	14	49
Bret Hedican	69	0	12	12	64
Gerald Diduck	55	1	10	11	72
Adrien Plavsic	47	1	9	10	6
John McIntyre	62	3	6	9	38
Tim Hunter	56	3	4	7	171
Nathan LaFayette	49	3	4	7	18
Dane Jackson	12	5	1	6	9
Dan Kesa	19	2	4	6	18
John Namestnikov	17	0	5	5	10
Neil Eisenhut	13	1	3	4	21
Kirk McLean	52	0	4	4	2
Shawn Antoski	55	1	2	3	190
Stephane Morin	5	1	1	2	6
Mike Peca	4	0	0	0	2
Kay Whitmore	32	0	0	0	6

THE GOALIES	GP	AVE	SO	RECORD
Kirk McLean	52	2.99	3	23-26-3
Kay Whitmore	32	3.53	0	18-14-0

PLAYOFFS

GP	W	L	T	GF	GA	PTS	PCT
24	15	9	0	76	61	—	.625

SCORING	GP	G	A	PTS	PIM
Pavel Bure	24	16	15	31	40
Trevor Linden	24	12	13	25	18
Geoff Courtnall	24	9	10	19	51
Jeff Brown	24	6	9	15	37
Cliff Ronning	24	5	10	15	16
Greg Adams	23	6	8	14	2
Murray Craven	22	4	9	13	18
Jyrki Lumme	24	2	11	13	16
Martin Gelinas	24	5	4	9	14
Nathan LaFayette	20	2	7	9	4
Dave Babych	24	3	5	8	12
Gerald Diduck	24	1	7	8	22
Bret Hedican	24	1	6	7	16
Sergio Momesso	24	3	4	7	56
Brian Glynn	17	0	3	3	10
Shawn Antoski	16	0	1	1	36
Jimmy Carson	2	0	1	1	0
Joe Charbonneau	3	1	0	1	4
John McIntyre	24	0	1	1	16
Kirk McLean	24	0	1	1	0
Tim Hunter	24	0	0	0	26
Dana Murzyn	7	0	0	0	4
Gino Odjick	10	0	0	0	18

THE GOALIES	GP	AVE	SO	RECORD
Kirk McLean	24	2.29	4	15-9-0

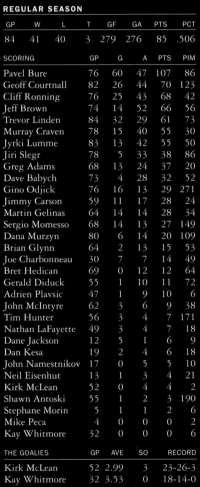

OPUS PRODUCTIONS INC.

President/Creative Director: Derik Murray
Designer: Dave Mason, Dave Mason & Associates
Design/Production Assistant: Pamela Lee, Dave Mason & Associates
Visual Coordinator: Victor John Penner
Assistant Visual Coordinator: Cathy Love
Artifact Photography Coordinator: Andreanne Ricard
Artifact Photography: Derik Murray Photography Inc./
Perry Danforth, Grant Waddell, Jason Stroud

Vice President, Sales and Marketing: Glenn McPherson
Marketing Coordinator: David Attard
Marketing Consultant: Tom Sponarski

Vice President, Director of Publishing: Marthe Love
Project Coordinator: Wendy Darling
Production Manager: Paula Guise
Special Research Consultant: Andrew Castell
Proofreader: Audrey Grescoe
Editorial Assistant: Robin Evans
Project Accountant: Kim Steele
Administrative Assistant: Karin Watson

Author: Sean Rossiter
Foreword: Jim Robson
Editor: Katherine Zmetana

*Opus Productions would like to thank the management and staff of the Vancouver Canucks
for their dedication and invaluable contribution to the project, especially the following:*
Arthur Griffiths, Chairman, Chief Executive Officer and Governor
Glen Ringdal, Vice President and Director of Marketing and Communications
Norm Jewison, Director of Publishing
Steve Frost, Director of Hockey Information
Melodi Kitagawa, Executive Assistant

Opus Productions appreciates the support of the following:
Raymond G. Dagg, President, The Western Information Network
John Plul, Vice President, Director of Marketing, CKNW
Lynn Munro, Director of Promotions and Community Relations, The Vancouver Sun and Province

*Opus Productions would like to acknowledge the staff of the Hockey Hall of Fame
for their cooperation and support, especially* Phil Pritchard, Manager, Resource Centre and Acquisitions.

Opus Productions is grateful to the following individuals and institutions for their assistance and support :
Pat Armstrong, B.C. Sports Hall of Fame • Cathy Best, Almyra Chow, Kent Sutherland, General Motors Place • Allan Black• Kim Blanchette,
Cilla Bachop, H. MacDonald Printing Company • Karen Carpenter, Sports Illustrated • Andrew Castell • Alan Clark, Karen Laurin, CBC Sports
• Ward Glassmeyer, National Hockey League • Joanne Griffiths, Canuck Foundation • Ron Harrison, Kelly Killby, Molstar Communications
• Alex Klenman, Can-Am Card Co. • Christine Leonard, Kim Smythe, Canuck Place • Jim Robson • Ray Scoffins, Scoffs Hockey Shop

AUTHOR'S NOTE

I would like to acknowledge the following for their enthusiasm and support: Norm Jewison, with whom I have had the privilege
to work often since he joined the club in 1977; Jim Robson, whose incomparable firsthand insight into the team after having seen and described every
game was especially valuable; Andrew Castell, known to many as the Canucks' Superfan and acknowledged by the Canucks' front office as the only human
being who knows more about the team than they do. *Towels, Triumph & Tears,* by Tony Gallagher and Mike Gasher, was a valuable reference for this project.
Notwithstanding their thoroughgoing efforts, the responsibility for those errors of fact and judgement that remain is mine alone.

SEAN ROSSITER

PHOTOGRAPHY CREDITS

Baglow, Glenn/*Vancouver Sun*: 108 bottom left; B. C. Sports Hall of Fame: 24 (puck), 29; Beck, Robert: front cover - top left, top right, bottom right, 10, 22 below, 66, 73, 79 top, 92 bottom left, 93 centre; Beck, Robert/*S.I.*: 89 below; Bosch, Steve/*Vancouver Sun*: 93 bottom; Bower, Ralph/*Vancouver Sun*: 47; Bruce Bennett Studios: 52, 60 bottom right, 67 top, 79 bottom left, 87, 88 top, 93 top; Buston, Dave/Canapress Photo Service: 16 bottom, 17 below; Canapress Photo Service: 27 bottom, 33; Courtesy of Canuck Place: 106; Davis, Stuart/*Vancouver Sun*: 108 centre/bottom right; Derik Murray Photography: 5, 105; Giamundo, J./Bruce Bennett Studios: 88 bottom, 89 above,

91; Hockey Hall of Fame: 34/35; Iacono, John/*S.I.*: 59 bottom; James, Glenn: 18 top right; Kallberg, Kent: 97 top, 103; Klutho, David E./*S.I.*: 18 top left, 86, 94/95, 96, 97 bottom, 98/99, 102 above; MacLellan, Doug/HHOF: 20 top, 20 bottom, 21 above, 92 top left, 100, 101 top; McLean B./Bruce Bennett Studios: 18 bottom left; Miller, Peter Read/*S.I.*: 60 bottom left; Molstar Communications/National Hockey League: 11; Murray, Derik: 43 bottom, 59 centre, 60 top, 61 bottom; Courtesy of Niagara Frontier Hockey L.P.: 27 top; Perrin, Ward/Canapress Photo Service: 17 above; Portnoy, Lewis/SpectrA-Action: back cover - top left, 26, 30, 32, 42 top right,

44/45; Relke, C. J.: front cover - bottom left, 3, 13, 14 top left, 14 bottom left, 14 bottom right, 15 top, 15 centre, 19 bottom, 20 centre, 22 above, 23 centre, 74/75, 80/81, 82 top left, 82 bottom right, 108 top left, top centre left, top centre right; Ridewood, Mike/ Canapress Photo Service: 16 top; Strohmeyer, Damian/*S.I.*: 102 below; Tomsic, Tony/*S.I.*: 59 top; Courtesy of the Vancouver Canucks: back cover - top centre left, top centre right, top right, bottom, 2, 6, 14 top right, 15 bottom, 18 bottom right, 19 top, 21 below, 23 top, 23 bottom, 24 top, 38, 39, 40, 41, 42 top left, 42 bottom left, 42 bottom right, 43 top, 48, 49, 53, 54, 55, 56, 61 top, 62, 63,

67 bottom left, 67 bottom right, 68, 69, 70, 71, 72, 76, 77, 78, 79 bottom right, 82 top right, 82 bottom left, 83, 90, 92 top right, 92 bottom right, 101 bottom, 104, 107, 108 top right, centre/top left, centre/top right, centre/bottom left, bottom/centre left, bottom/ center right, bottom right; UPI/Bettmann: 58.
*S.I. = Sports Illustrated

We would like to acknowledge the following Vancouver Canucks photographers whose work is represented in this book: Chris Bickford, Bill Cunningham, Kent Kallberg, Wayne Leidenfrost, Derik Murray, Jack Murray.

SELECT BIBLIOGRAPHY

Andrews, Ron, ed., Jewison, Norm and Randall, Carol, assoc eds. *National Hockey League Guide, 1970-71 to 1980-81*, pub by the NHL. • Boyd, Denny. *The Vancouver Canucks Story*, Toronto, McGraw-Hill Ryerson Ltd., 1973. • Douglas, Greg; Jewison, Norman, and others, *Vancouver Canucks Yearbook,* *1969-70 to 1993-94.* • Gallagher, Tony and Gasher, Mike. *Towels, Triumph & Tears*, Madiera Park, Harbour Publishing Co. Ltd., 1982. • Imlach, Punch with Young, Scott. *Heaven and Hell in the NHL,* Toronto, McClelland and Stewart, 1983 ed. • Jewison, Norman (photographs by Bill Cunningham). *Vancouver Canucks: The First Twenty Years*, Nelson B.C., Polestar Press Ltd., 1990. • Whitehead, Eric. *Cyclone Taylor, A Hockey Legend*, Toronto, Doubleday Canada Ltd., 1977. • Williams, Tiger, with Lawton, James. *Tiger: A Hockey Story*, Vancouver, Douglas & McIntyre, 1984.

• *The author gratefully acknowledges the information provided in interviews for this book with the following:* Norm Jewison, Rick Ley, Trevor Linden, Mickey McDowell, Kirk McLean, Phil Maloney, Harry Neale, Mike Penny, Pat Quinn, Gary Smith, Ron Smith, Stan Smyl, Dave "Tiger" Williams.

• *The author also made use of material from profiles written by himself for various publications from 1975 to 1992, including* Breakaway!, The Georgia Straight, Vancouver Magazine, Vancouver Canucks Hockey Magazine *and* Weekend *magazine, about the following:* Greg Adams, Garth Butcher, Richard Brodeur, Arthur Griffiths, Glen Hanlon, Vladimir Krutov, Igor Larionov, Pat Quinn, Kirk McLean, Doug Lidster, Jake Milford, Harry Neale, Roger Neilson, Barry Pederson, Jim Robson, Jim Sandlak, Gary Smith, Rich Sutter, Mike Walton, Steve Weeks and others.